Middle School
and the
Age of Adjustment

Middle School
and the
Age of Adjustment

❖❖

A Guide for Parents

Eileen Bernstein

BERGIN & GARVEY
Westport, Connecticut • London

MT

Library of Congress Cataloging-in-Publication Data

Bernstein, Eileen, 1941–
   Middle school and the age of adjustment : a guide for parents / Eileen Bernstein.
      p.   cm.
   Includes bibliographical references and index.
   ISBN 0–89789–906–7 (alk. paper)
      1. Middle school education—Parent participation—Handbooks, manuals, etc.   2.
   Adolescent psychology—Handbooks, manuals, etc.   I. Title.
   LB1623.B48   2002
   373.236—dc21   2002018212

British Library Cataloguing in Publication Data is available.

Library of Congress Catalog Card Number: 2002018212
ISBN: 0–89789–906–7

First published in 2002

Bergin & Garvey, 88 Post Road West, Westport, CT 06881
An imprint of Greenwood Publishing Group, Inc.
www.greenwood.com

Printed in the United States of America

∞™

The paper used in this book complies with the
Permanent Paper Standard issued by the National
Information Standards Organization (Z39.48–1984).

10 9 8 7 6 5 4 3 2 1

7/12/04

Contents

Introduction

Sex. Drugs. Puberty. Algebra. These are just a few of the problems that parents have to worry about when their eleven-year-old walks through the doors of middle school. The eleven-year-old, meanwhile, has to be brave in a scary new world filled with constant change that creates self-doubt and emotional turmoil. The child has just come from fifth grade, king or queen of the hill, in a warm, sheltered environment. Now, in middle school, these new sixth graders are peewees on a school bus, sitting with teenage boys who may be shaving already and girls with well-developed bodies. The teenagers tell the sixth graders where to sit, and there is no choice because the older children are bigger and stronger.

I am a middle school counselor, and I have been helping these children make their way through this difficult emotional minefield. I have written this book for parents to describe this rapidly changing time and give advice to help in their child's adjustment. As a counselor and teacher for nearly thirty years, I have watched class after class of middle schoolers experience this very difficult period in their lives. Changes in our society have deeply affected these young adolescent boys and girls.

School buildings and their occupants have changed dramatically over the last half-century. In the 1940s and '50s, elementary schools were comprised of grades K–8, and children walked home for lunch. As the population grew in the country, junior highs for grades 7–9 were developed because elementary schools began to bulge at the seams. But a problem developed in the new junior highs: ninth graders did not take their grades seriously because they were still in junior high. This lack of academic seriousness can impact the overall grade point average, affecting college choice. In addition, high schools offer sports and other activities, which also enhance college entrance possibilities and could lead to scholarships. It is much better for high schools to include grades 9–12, so that students can be more serious about how their education affects their future educational choices.

Thus, high schools became grades 9–12, and many communities developed the intermediate school, which includes seventh and eighth grade, although some communities still had junior high schools. As the school age population mushroomed, the middle school, comprised of grades 6–8, was created. Now, sixth grade, which was formerly in elementary school, is combined with the seventh and eighth grades, a time when hormones quickly develop. Currently, this trend is growing. In the past few years, however, middle schools have come to be thought of as a middle child: difficult to understand, in need of attention (but what kinds of attention?), and extremely variable in behavior.

With the recent advent of terrible acts of violence in high schools and middle schools, it is important to understand who the middle school child is. Much has been written about adolescence, the journey from childhood to adulthood. But middle school children are young adolescents when they enter in sixth grade and full-blown adolescents when they leave in eighth grade. It is in middle school that social problems and painful rejection can occur. This can lead to the feeling of alienation that some high school children have felt when they have brought guns to school and killed their classmates.

The purpose of this book is to help parents understand the middle school child as he or she is growing up in a technological, media-obsessed, lack-of-extended-family society. Middle school children are at great risk today because they have unmonitored time to experiment with drugs and sex. However, whether you are a single parent or living in an intact marriage, you can have tremendous influence in guiding children successfully through these difficult and complex middle school years.

SERIOUS ISSUES OF EARLY ADOLESCENCE

1. There is an increase in unsupervised time between the end of school and the time that parents get home in the evening.

2. Many children are not comfortable reading and learning because they have been entertained excessively.

3. When children do not spend time doing homework and participating in enriching activities, they often feel bored.

4. There is early experimentation with sexual activity, to which children have been exposed in movies and on television.

5. There is easy access to alcohol and drugs accompanied by peer pressure to experience intoxication.

6. Because families are not located in the same community, there is a lessening of the strong family influence that existed in past generations.

7. Television may provide children with role models who do not inspire goal setting and achievement.

8. Our country has developed an emphasis on materialism as a main value, which creates a focus on short-term rewards and a need for more money.

9. Guns are easily purchased, which is causing some incidents of serious violence in the schools.

10. There is a lack of traditional values, such as honesty, helpfulness, and diligence, which give children meaningful goals and help them to monitor their own behavior.

11. There is an overall lessening of responsibility by parents to monitor and guide their children and by children to follow rules and to be good students.

12. There is a need for schools to take a more active role in helping children with their social and emotional problems.

13. Parents should find support systems in the neighborhood and the community to help monitor and guide their children.

Chapter 1

Who Is a Middle School Child?

Do you remember the first three years of your child's life? He or she went from being a newborn to a walking, talking, I-have-my-own-ideas child.

You can draw a similar comparison with middle school children. They start out at the age of eleven, in sixth grade, which used to be in elementary school. They enter sixth grade full of apprehension, encountering enormous change in their daily school lives.

One afternoon I went to talk about middle school to the fifth graders. I knew the one question that they would always ask: Do eighth graders stuff sixth graders in lockers? Of course, the children did not know that the lockers were not big enough and that the school disciplines students for aggressive behavior anyway.

The children were full of questions. What kind of food is sold in the lunchroom? What sports are played in physical education? How much homework is there? What do you do if the older kids pick on you at the bus stop? What kind of notebook should you have? What is a seven-period day like? Do you have to change in PE? They felt great excitement about coming to middle school, but they were also full of fears. I made sure to take a long time to try to allay their fears because I knew they had so many!

I vividly remember this experience:

The first day of school, Mrs. Floyd, the math teacher, brought Camille to my office. Camille was crying. After talking to Camille for a while and finding no reason for the crying, I called her mother, but she had no explanation, either. Camille cried every day for two weeks. Then it stopped. She had finally adjusted to middle school. I know that some children take longer to adjust than others.

Middle school students leave at the age of thirteen or fourteen, full of raging hormones and having the answer to everything. The changes in those three years mirror the changes in the first three years of their lives because there are so many changes in such a short period of time.

Early adolescents experience tremendous changes in three areas of their lives: physical, social, and emotional. Take a look at sixth graders. A girl can be tiny, not having reached puberty, or she can be physically developed, looking like a sixteen-year-old. Puberty for girls can start as early as age nine—yes—or as late as age fourteen. A girl's strong interest in a boy often correlates with her physical development. More troubling is the fact that once a girl becomes physically developed, boys notice her and often make sexual comments, even to a nine-year-old. This can be very disturbing to a young girl, and she often does not know how to react appropriately. Parents of these girls must teach them to react to boys in an assertive manner by looking directly at them and telling them to stop, and to ask for help from school officials if comments and actions don't stop.

What about boys? They do not vary quite as much until they reach the age of twelve. Then they can be small, still boy-like, or they can be starting puberty with changes in their bodies and voices. Boys in middle school, until eighth grade, often do not care about their appearance. They have to be reminded to brush their teeth and take a shower. They often don't care what clothes they are wearing, dirty or clean. This can be very irritating to parents, who have higher standards. A sense of humor can be invaluable when this happens.

Go to a middle school dance and you will be amazed at how kids can range in appearance from children to adolescents. Girls are often taller than boys until eighth grade. Those who mature faster obviously develop a stronger interest in the opposite sex. The opposite sex may or may not return the interest.

At her first experience as a parent chaperone, Mrs. Jordan watched the children in amusement. She described to me how the younger children were running around in groups for the whole evening, talking and giggling. Some of the younger boys didn't even talk to the girls. A few eighth graders were dancing. They all really liked the group dances, and the children were myriad sizes and shapes. I knew that it was a lot of noisy activity and that high school dances looked very different from this.

As girls mature, they become obsessed with their bodies. Are they developing properly? Should they lie and tell other girls that they got their period? Their information about their own sexuality varies tremendously, depending on whether their mothers talk openly to them. Girls also are often prey to sexual harassment from boys and also from other girls. References are made to their breast size, and often their bra straps are pulled.

Barbara came to my office in tears. She was a well-developed girl who had reached puberty early. This was the second day of school and she said that on the bus, several boys offered her a dollar if she would let them touch her breasts. I had to let her cry for a while before I could begin to talk to her. Eventually, she became calmer. I tried to console her and explained that she was correct in coming to me. After we talked for a while, I called her mother. We would have to work on identifying the boys involved. I also suggested that she try to accompany the girls at the bus stop and on the bus. This would provide some protection.

Girls do not know what to make of this negative attention. Even though they may be taught that sexual harassment is wrong, they want to be noticed and popular, so they do not want to complain. They do not understand the line between flirting, which shows mutual interest, and sexual harassment, which is degrading and unwanted. So, students often are called to the office to answer claims of sexual harassment. The adults work with them daily to explain the difference between acceptable and inappropriate behavior.

Imagine this scene: As Mr. Baker was walking around the room, he saw that Kira looked upset. When he approached her desk, he saw that she was sitting in a small puddle of blood. Being a father of daughters, he knew immediately what had happened. He directed the entire class to leave the room to go to the library (the librarian had no idea, of course). He asked Kira to leave last and to turn out the lights, giving her an opportunity to go to the health room to get supplies for her first menstrual period.

Gym classes require that students change clothes so that sweaty clothing is not worn in the classroom. This means that children have to bring a change of clothing to school and take it home to be washed on a regular basis. This is another adjustment for many girls.

Kelly asked her English teacher if she could see me. She wanted to know if she could be allowed not to change for physical education, or PE. When I asked her why, she said that she was very embarrassed to take her shirt off in front of other people. I remembered what a PE teacher told me once: she could wear two tee shirts to school and take off the top one in the locker room. Afterwards, she could change tops in the bathroom. She said that she would try this.

Just about all girls in middle school go through puberty. What about boys? They have a much longer span for their growth and change. Most boys begin to have observable major puberty changes starting in seventh grade. But they may complete their physical journey well into high school. Boys in middle school still retain their boyish characteristics. They like to run, to be physical. They seem to need to keep moving.

Mr. Michaels, assistant principal, always had to ask the sixth-grade boys to stop running as they were going to lunch. It was interesting how the eighth-grade boys did not run. The sixth graders were full of energy and they were very physical. The eighth graders were more interested in socializing. They would usually saunter to class.

Eighth grade marks the biggest change. Many boys are developed sexually, which makes eighth grade the hotbed of hormones:

Tim had been shy since he entered middle school. Sometimes a teacher would come to me because Tim did not want to give oral reports in class. I had worked with him over the years, having him practice in front of me, which helped. When he came to me in eighth grade about a PE problem, I was saddened by what he said. He hesitated to change clothes in eighth grade because now the boys were talking about who had the largest penis. Knowing that he would have to adjust to another challenge, I tried to make him see the situation in a humorous way, and to go along with the exaggeration of the boys. Meanwhile, I made a note to tell the PE teacher about the latest absurdity.

With the sexual messages and permissiveness that our society fosters today, eighth grade becomes the real time for risk-taking behaviors. Thus, in middle school the physical changes abound, creating a circus of sizes and shapes of development.

Next come the social changes. In elementary school, children usually have a set of friends that they have had for years. These friendships are often arranged by their parents either because of geographical desirability or because of specific interests. Girls in particular form fast friendships because they are very relationship-oriented. Boys tend to form relationships through sports, computers, or video games. Neighborhoods determine their friendships.

Middle school changes all of that. Often, two to three or more elementary schools converge to form a middle school. This means that everyone is meeting new classmates. Some of these new children are very popular or have a strong social presence. This sets the stage for changes in friendships, especially for girls. Even though there are cliques in elementary school, the cliques that form in middle school are stronger because there is increasing power over more classmates. It is always a challenge for me to talk to these girls and encourage them to understand the hurt feelings that often develop with these social problems.

Sarah was used to being a central figure in her fifth-grade class. But after a week in sixth grade, she saw that she had power not only over her friends and some new girls, but she was also popular with many seventh and eighth graders whom she knew in elementary school. After a month in middle school, some friends called her the "queen" of the school. She began to use her power in a negative way, demanding homework answers from the smart girls, who would then complain to me about the intimidation. Working with young adolescents who have new power in middle school requires a great deal of patience from the adults because they must explain the impact of behaviors to the children and maintain a policy of what is right and what is not acceptable.

Sometimes, girls become devastated as they watch their best friends moving away from them and forming new friendships. The socially stronger girls enlarge their influence and hang around new girls as the socially weaker girls watch them move away from them. This change and stress can bring verbal aggression in girls. One of the biggest problems in middle school arises when girls call each other foul names or spread vicious gossip about other girls. They often write notes to each other full of name-calling words—"bitch" and "ho" are the biggest. Sometimes, they become excessively nasty and call a girl a lesbian. Then rumors spread, and some girls end up in tears.

Why do girls do this? This is their outlet of aggression as they form new pecking orders in a new social environment. Many girls become obsessed with this new, fluctuating social order, and some become depressed when they are left out.

When Charlene burst into tears because her best friend was ignoring her, I planned a conference where she could express her feelings about being left out of her friend's new social group. Then I asked the friend to define the relationship as she wanted it to be. It was always a tricky conference to hold because you can't force friendships on people. This time, the girls decided to keep their friendship, and Charlene agreed to make some new friends. I was relieved that the conference ended well, and I called Charlene's mom. I told Charlene that I would do this.

How do boys change socially? Boys, too, are now introduced to other students from other schools. Boys' popularity usually centers around athletic ability. Being good in sports gives boys a great sense of confidence. The opposite is true for the nonathletic boys. They often are teased, and they know that they are lacking an essential skill that makes them popular in school. Boys also make changes in friendships, but not as dramatically as girls do. That is because boys usually have far fewer friends. Often two or three friends are par for boys. The social scene is set by eighth grade for the popular boys and girls to start to come together in risk-taking behaviors.

Lunchtime in middle school is a noisy, social arena. There are basic rules for behavior and cleanliness, but there aren't enough adults to keep their eyes on the kids. In our old building, we had a single bathroom next to the lunchroom, and this had a lock on the inside. One day, the assistant principal happened to see Jodie and Mel leave the bathroom at the same time. Of course, they were immediately whisked up to the office. After being questioned separately, it was apparent that they were engaging in some kind of sexual activity. The principal decided to post one of the building service workers outside that bathroom in the future.

Basically, middle school is an arena for learning more complex social skills. Boys and girls are often awkward socially, and they often choose to say negative things to each other to avoid the feeling of awkwardness. They experiment with friendships with different people as they begin to see more choices in their lives. The axiom of taking two steps forward and one step back applies to the acquisition of social skills. You never know when a misunderstanding will develop between friends or children who are not friends. Meanwhile, all of the staff becomes involved as they are helping children to learn positive social skills. Whether it takes place in the administrator's office, the counselor's office, or the classroom, teaching acceptable behavior is a constant in middle school.

And what are the emotional changes that these physical and social changes bring about? It is the beginning of the roller coaster ride of emotions that middle school children experience. No one is immune to this. Imagine questioning yourself daily: do you look right, do you act right, did you say something stupid, are people looking at you, did you wear the right clothes today? Young adolescents begin the total self-absorption that will be a major characteristic of their lives until they reach adulthood. When parents ask questions and try to help, they may get a barrage of anger or a flood of tears—they cannot fathom how their child can change moods so rapidly.

When Sally came home from school and her mother asked her how her day was, Sally ran up the stairs crying and slammed the door as she went into her room. Sally's mom didn't know whether to try to comfort her or to wait until Sally became calmer. Sometimes Sally would not share what was bothering her, but other times she would be very open. The problem was always what someone said about her. And Sally listened to the gossip. She did not have the courage to confront the person who supposedly spread rumors about her, and she begged her mother not to call me. Sally's mother never knew what the best thing to do was, so she just tried to make Sally feel better by planning an activity that Sally liked. Later, Sally's mom called me to share what had happened, and she asked me to keep an eye on her daughter to be sure that she was all right. I knew that "all right" would not last long because these problems continually resurface.

Sometimes, middle schoolers do not want to come to school, or they may develop stomachaches. If this is persistent, there could be serious adjustment problems, and the school counselor should be consulted.

Sandy was the second daughter of the Miller family. Her sister Alice had been my counselee, and she had few problems with middle school. Mrs. Miller was grateful for the good relationship that she and I had because Sandy was having a rough time adjusting to sixth grade. She had a lot of stomachaches and headaches, and she started to refuse to go to school. We had a long conference where I asked Sandy to tell me how she felt about school and what was difficult for her. We worked out a compromise where Mrs. Miller agreed to drive Sandy to school because the bus scene was the most difficult for her to deal with. I wanted Mrs. Miller to know that it was very important that she not allow Sandy to develop school phobia, which can be a challenge to treat.

All parents worry as they watch their children go through the pain of adjustment. A few children are spared the painful swing of emotions. Those children are usually born with very adaptive temperaments.

So, a middle schooler is a person who will enter sixth grade as a child, emerge two years later as an adolescent, and will go through tremendous changes. Sometimes, a child can change from day to day. Middle school is very exciting to most students, with the change to a seven-period day and more freedom. But they are also being weaned from one teacher who really cares to seven teachers who really care but have 150 students to care about. The physical, social, and emotional changes are always present in the mind of a middle school child. The requirements for adapting can be daunting. Throw in the higher academic requirements and the organizational responsibilities, and you will see children who are struggling to make sense of their world.

Chapter 2

Adjustment to Sixth Grade

Sixth grade used to be in elementary school. That was a wonderful time for many children because there were certain privileges. You could be a patrol guard for the buses, or, even better, you could be a patrol captain. Some sixth graders raised and lowered the flag daily, and some did morning announcements.

In middle school, sixth grade is very different. Students change from having one elementary teacher at the beginning and end of the day, with, perhaps, another math or social studies teacher, to having seven teachers daily in middle school. The first-period teacher is not the last-period teacher. There is no one at the end of the day to remind children about what they need for the next day.

There are so many adjustments. Take lockers, for example. The first day of school, children have to be able to open a combination lock. If parents have not prepared them for this task, simple as it may be, it can be daunting to a new sixth grader and it may cause tears.

During the opening homeroom on the first day of school, the sixth-grade teachers were overwhelmed with calls for help from students who did not know how to open a combination lock. Even though there was a summer orientation at school, not all students attended, so some could not open a lock. They were so frustrated and scared! The teachers were used to this and went patiently from one student to another. I tried to help as much as I could, but my phone was ringing constantly with calls from parents who were worried about their sixth graders, and I needed to assuage their fears.

At age eleven, children now must adjust to seven teachers, seven personality types. Even if every teacher was a model of patience and helpfulness, adjusting to seven authority figures takes some time. For example, Mrs. A. may post the homework on the front board, and Mr. B. may post homework on the sideboard. As simple as this may sound, it is difficult for some eleven-year-olds to think expansively enough to adjust to this.

At our weekly team meetings, when the academic teachers and I met, we discussed student problems and parent concerns. Mrs. Lerner had called me about the difficulty that Martha had in writing down homework assignments. I decided to ask each teacher exactly when and where homework was posted. There certainly was no commonality in the process. Some teachers are more organized than others, or some math teachers may want to see how far they get in a period before deciding on homework. It is not a simple process. We brainstormed ideas to try to standardize the process to help the students.

One of the major challenges for these children is becoming well-organized. Now a notebook has five sections for their academic subjects. There may be an assignment book, a separate spiral notebook where students write down the homework. They also may use these notebooks for passes. Many children cannot find last night's homework, or they leave their books in the locker when they go home because they do not remember that they have homework in a specific subject. Parents become so frustrated because they saw Johnny doing his math homework, yet they got a call from the teacher saying that the homework was not turned in.

Mrs. Adams called me to ask if there was someone who could check Johnny's backpack at the end of the day to be sure that all of his books were there. Unfortunately, with 300 students in the sixth-grade class, there was no one who could check each of the 300 students at the end of the day. Some parents had a difficult time adjusting to the fact that their child had to become organized and responsible. They missed that hand-holding that elementary school teachers give. Sometimes, parents are rude to the school staff because there is not a quick solution to this problem. I tell parents that I will let the teachers know of their concern about their child and that home help in organization skills is a must.

One of the pleasures for athletic middle school children is that they have physical education every day. But this, too, brings adjustments. They must have their own combination lock to put on their gym locker because they must change clothes for gym. This requires memorizing two locker combinations. They have to remember to bring their gym clothes and to take them home to be washed as well. Sometimes, there is a trek from the gym to their next class, where a tardy could give them a lunch detention. More changes! Some children have difficulty changing clothes in front of others, but if they don't change clothes, their grade drops. The students who are not athletic encounter more teasing. The PE class can be a positive or negative experience. Parents need to know all of these details about middle school so that they can work with teachers to solve problems.

In fact, change is the name of the game in sixth grade. While the children are adjusting on a daily basis in the beginning, they are bringing home their excitement, fears, and concerns, and the new teachers, counselors, and administrators are just getting to know these children and their parents. There are always special needs cases, such as children with attention deficit disorder (ADD) or those who are learning disabled. All of the adults are communicating to help the children, but it takes time for all to get to know and understand each other.

Mrs. Baker called the first week of school. She wanted to be sure that Billy was sitting in the front of all of his academic classes and that the teachers knew of his needs. He had a 504 Plan, which is a document that gives accommodations to children who have a specifically documented condition that interferes with learning or other major life functions. Billy was easily distracted, and he needed the teacher to help him focus on the assignment. The only problem for the teachers was that several other students in their classes had ADD, and there were only so many front seats. I told Mrs. Baker that I would remind the teachers of this accommodation.

An interesting phenomenon occurs in sixth grade. Sometimes, elementary teachers report that a specific child has been a behavior problem. When that child enters sixth grade, he or she may love the constant change of classes and teachers, and there may be no behavior problem. However, a child who thrived with one teacher's special attention in elementary school may become a behavior problem in sixth grade because he or she needs that special attention. What this really shows is that you cannot predict how any sixth grader will adjust. And since middle school is full of change, from year to year, any student may become more or less successful socially or academically.

Mrs. Lowden, an English teacher, asked me to find out about Mary. For several weeks Mary had been almost clinging to her. Mary would ask questions after class every day and she would raise her hand often during class work to ask for extra help. I called Mary's elementary counselor and found that she always had been placed in the smallest classes possible because she was very insecure about her work. Her mother appeared to be a hypercritical person who put a lot of pressure on Mary. When I explained that to Mrs. Lowden, she said that she would try to be patient in getting Mary to be more independent.

Children really need a lot of guidance and monitoring from their parents while they are in middle school. There are various strategies that parents can use to help. For example, having a school calendar on the refrigerator where major assignments and tests are listed will constantly remind students that work is due. Making flash cards to learn information enables a child to test him or herself. Studying out loud for a test helps students to retain information. Children often do not know how to study at home for tests. Parents should help children to understand science and social studies textbooks. A lot of academic guidance is needed to prevent grades from dropping. Lack of achievement could become a chronic problem.

At one of our weekly team meetings, the teachers brought up Tom's name. His notebook was a mess with unorganized loose papers. He did have dividers, but he apparently didn't want to use them. When I met with him, Tom said that he didn't like to take the time to organize papers, that he wanted to do his work quickly and then go outside to play. I asked him if it would be OK for me to ask his mom to help him every weekend. I always asked my students for permission to call home unless I thought that it was imperative that I do so, and in that case I told them that I would have to call. Tom agreed to have his mom help him. When children resist a parent's help, an outside intermediary, such as a teacher or counselor, can influence children to acquire a new, positive strategy and work with their parents.

Most sixth graders eventually become very happy with the constant changes and the additional classes that they now have. They get to have an arts class as well as PE every day. Arts classes include such courses as art, home economics, tech education, TV lab, and others, and they can be a semester long each. Foreign language can be added in seventh grade. There is also the choice of adding a music course, such as band, orchestra, or chorus. Lunch is a time to socialize. There is more freedom as well as responsibility. There are school dances, and the cafeteria has a la carte items, which the students love. But for a small percentage of sixth graders, adjustment to middle school may take as long as a year. If the home and school keep communicating, progress can be made.

Chapter 3

Boys' Challenges

Although individual personality, environment, and heredity make each person unique, research using brain scans reveals that there are some basic differences between the male and female brain, as well as in male and female hormones. These basic differences account for the varying behaviors that we often see in males and females.

The predominant male hormone, testosterone, is a sex and aggression hormone. When testosterone develops in males, they experience several surges a day of this hormone. An aggression response is a domination response. When a male accidentally runs into a chair, his response will likely be to kick the chair. A girl will more likely reveal pain and cry. When a male suffers emotionally, he may act out aggressively. More males die from suicide attempts than females because males often do not know how to communicate feelings. Females usually use suicide attempts as a cry for help. Males will be more aggressive in their attempt to kill themselves. More males die throughout life from their aggression (Steve Biddulph, 1998).

How does this affect middle school behavior? In elementary school, there is plenty of aggression among all children, but there are fewer children in the building, and there are more controls in an elementary school, such as walking single file in the halls. In middle school, there are many more children, there is more physical independence in the halls and, therefore, more opportunity to act out aggressively before an adult can intervene.

Mike and Tom began to take each other's supplies in art class. Then, they began to call each other names. When the first boy made a comment about the other boy's mother, the fists started flying. Both boys ended up in the office of the assistant principal, and both were suspended for fighting. As is usual with boys, minor physical acts escalated into a fight. Why did they always have to insult each other's mother? I made a note to discuss this with them.

Boys love to push and shove and be physical, but this is a form of connecting, using aggressive behaviors rather than using words, which girls use, to bond. Most boys understand the give and take of physical behavior, and they regard this as a form of connecting. Teachers, however, are always aware that one push can get too rough, and the friendliness can turn into an altercation. Thus, teachers are often admonishing boys to stop fooling around. Those boys who do not like physical play often become the brunt of teasing because they show vulnerability.

Mrs. Grant called me because Alan came home from school crying after some boys pushed him on the bus. Of course, the administration would take care of trouble on the bus, but I knew that Alan would have a difficult time in middle school because he could not participate in the give and take of physical play engaged in by boys. I tried to explain this to Alan's mother, but I knew that mothers of the boys who had difficulty with this type of play were usually too sensitive to their child's complaints. I would have to work a lot with Alan to get him to be more relaxed in this boy's world.

A major difference in the brain of boys and girls is that verbal areas occur in both sides of the female brain but in only one side of the male brain (Christina Hoff Sommers, 2000). This means that it takes boys more time to process emotional information. They often do not know what they are feeling until a conversation brings it out. They also tend sometimes to act without thinking, which creates a problem in controlling impulsive behavior.

Even though Mark was given lunch detention every time he was impulsively aggressive, he still had trouble stopping the behavior that would get him in trouble. His mother could not figure this out. She would talk to him about self-control, but she even saw at home that Mark often failed to think about what he was doing. She worried that he might never change even though the assistant principal assured her that children do mature and learn to understand their behavior. When she called me to discuss this, I assured her that I often see a big difference in self-control as the children go through middle school. When we all work with them, even the most impulsive grow in their self-control.

Ability in spatial relations occupies a much larger part of the male brain than of the female brain. This explains boys' interest in tasks, projects, and sports. Their brains follow the trajectory of balls and the electronic games easily. Males originally hunted for food, which required them to follow moving objects. Many boys love to build structures. It appears that males often need to prove their worth, and society must provide systems to enable males to do this. Sports, of course, is a major outlet in which boys can excel, especially if they have difficulty learning or controlling impulsive behavior. Boys need positive outlets for their aggression.

Mrs. Hudson called me because Brian loved basketball and wanted to try out for the school team, but his low grades made him ineligible. I know that it is important for children to learn that extracurricular activities are a privilege that you earn from having good grades, but I also feel that in middle school, playing sports is a way to keep kids connected to school. I suggested that Mrs. Hudson meet with Brian and me. We would set up a contract where he would agree to do his homework daily, and then he could appeal his eligibility. I hoped that this would work, because I have seen some boys develop very negative attitudes when they were denied access to sports.

Once boys enter high school and approach the age of sixteen, they begin to see themselves as men, and they therefore plan for their future and think about grades and college. But in middle school, the maturity is not there. Keeping boys on a serious academic track is often challenging for schools and parents. Both need to work together constantly on strategies that enable boys to be academically successful. If a boy is not achieving for three years in middle school, his setback can seriously impair his desire to achieve in high school. Here is a strategy that teachers may use:

The seventh grade team of teachers met to discuss the fact that Len was not doing his homework. They had already had a parent conference, to no avail. They decided to meet with Len as a team and to tell him that he would have to miss his favorite subject, gym, to do his work for two days a week if he did not improve. They would get the gym teacher's approval first. Occasionally, the threat of missing a favorite activity on a short-term basis will motivate a student to improve. Sometimes the teachers could have a positive impact on students when they forced them to do work in school. However, without support at home, getting academic work done is very difficult. I would have to call the parents again.

If boys feel that they cannot live up to expectations, they often lose self-esteem and may develop dysfunctional behaviors (Lawrence Beymer, 1995). Boys need to have a vision, a definition of their future world. They need order and organization. Some boys join gangs in order to fulfill their need for order and a sense of self-worth. They need to be taught that life requires tenderness as well as toughness. To communicate with them, ask them what they think about concrete issues. Teach them how to use humor and language to avoid conflicts. To boys, a fight is not about winning; it's about respect. If they have strong self-respect, they will not need to defend their reputations as much.

Sometimes I cut out articles from the paper that I save to read to my counselees to make a point. I recently read an article about the boy who starred in a movie about a young teen who wanted to learn ballet. He said that kids made fun of him a lot when he started to take ballet lessons. But he loved dancing, and he knew that it would be his life's goal. He decided to totally ignore the teasing because he truly believed in himself; he still talked to the kids and acted as if everything was normal. After a while, when the other students saw he would not react to the teasing, they stopped. I wondered what it took for a young man to be so strong!

The great thing about boys in middle school is that they are very direct, and they say what they mean. If they think that an adult is really trying to help them with a problem, they will work in a direct manner with that adult. Sometimes they get emotional, but more often they will want to seek a solution and move forward.

When Danny and Matt were told that they would not be allowed to sit near each other on the bus because of their continual conflicts, they both decided to flip a coin to see who would sit at the front and who would sit at the back. They agreed to cooperate about this. When given a chance by the assistant principal to find a solution, they did. They were very objective in analyzing the problem.

As boys develop sexually, not only do they become interested in girls, but girls also become interested in them. However, girls today are much more aggressive in their pursuit of boys. Girls will call boys at all hours, and although the boys are flattered, their parents become upset with this out-of-bounds behavior. Parents today need to talk to their sons about sexuality, appropriate behavior, and boundaries. The interests of boys and girls often collide in that girls want a relationship, and boys are more often just interested in sex. Parents need to help boys to keep a level head about these new temptations.

In the middle of the year, I had a new enrollee. Troy was a very handsome and affable young man in the eighth grade. When I mentioned that the girls must be calling him, he smiled, and his mom proceeded to tell me how relentless some of the girls were, calling at all hours. I reminded Troy that there would be plenty of time in his life for girls and that his education would give him some great choices for his future. I pulled mom aside and suggested that Troy's dad have a lot of conversations with him about girls from a dad's point of view. Mom should talk to him also.

Because many boys like to be physical in order to confirm their masculinity (Lawrence Beymer, 1995), it is important for parents to be sure that they are kept busy with their favorite activities. After-school programs are very helpful to boys. Parents need to monitor them because some boys like risk-taking activities. Eighth grade particularly is the age of experimentation with alcohol, drugs, and sex. The unattended hours after school are particularly dangerous hours when some boys will seek to end their boredom by trying things that can harm them.

In addition, by eighth grade, adolescents with common interests seek each other out. The computer kids find each other, the kids in music programs tend to seek each other out, and the kids experimenting with alcohol and drugs find one other. The kids who are angry because of home problems know each other, and they join in their anger to do things that are rebellious. If there are no positive interventions at this time, these students, boys and girls, are headed for big trouble.

Carl and John had been angry for several years because their fathers had left the home and did not communicate with them. Even though their mothers tried to fill the hole, the boys would not cooperate and had no interest in achieving in school, even though they were capable. They knew where to buy drugs and they were talking about a secret place where they could hang out and have fun. When their teachers tried to talk to them, they just blew it off.

Boys need a father to teach them to be men. Boys love to be with their fathers, and if their fathers are "no good," then boys may subconsciously believe that they are probably no good also. This can become a prophecy fulfilled if there are no positive male role models in a boy's life to show him love. It is also important to note that violence is a learned form of behavior. If a boy grows up seeing his father hitting his mother, he may very likely imitate this behavior when he forms dating relationships. So, boys need positive and responsible males to teach them.

Boys (and girls) need to be taught problem-solving skills. Boys in groups need order and structure or they will vie for a pecking order (Steve Biddulph, 1998). Often, when boys are bothered by something, they will act out before thinking. They need to be taught to think through problems and analyze various solutions.

Jason thought that the bus driver kept staring at him. He would see the driver smiling at other times, but the driver did not seem to smile at him. Finally, out of frustration, Jason cussed at the driver. When the administrator had to deal with this, he asked Jason why he never brought up this perception to an adult at school. Jason did not know why, which revealed that he had very poor problem-solving skills. Instead of thinking about the problem, he just acted impulsively.

Boys are full of promise. They can grow up to build bridges, to paint pictures, to become loving men, and to accomplish any goal. They need positive role models at home and a connection between school and home to keep them on the right track. They need adults to understand their needs and to teach them positive problem-solving.

Chapter 4

Girls' Challenges

Girls' brains develop differently from those of boys. The area of girls' brains involving verbal ability and relationship interests develops faster. This makes girls at an early age interested in playing with dolls. They talk to their dolls and they also play in such a way that the dolls have relationships with each other. Girls also begin to develop hormones at age six, which creates temperamental behavior earlier than one sees in boys.

By the time girls get to middle school, they are experts in childhood relationships. But conditions change dramatically in middle school. All children develop the ability to reason at about age nine (Jean Piaget, 2000). By age eleven, when they converge in middle school, adjusting to changes in friendships becomes of paramount concern to girls. They are meeting new girls and forming new relationships. Jealousies abound. Girls can become very aggressive verbally and in notes they frequently write. They can't wait to get home to get on the phone to discuss the day's events and who said what about whom.

Betty had a conference call, but Holly didn't know this. Betty called Sarah and they plotted for Sarah to be quiet while Betty called Holly to ask her what she thought of Sarah. When Holly said that she thought that Sarah was fat, a huge confrontation developed the next day. Betty felt a surge of power because she was in control of these relationships, and I had a crying girl to deal with. When I talked to Betty and Sarah, I would have to be careful to stress empathy and understanding so that I would not sound like a parent or administrator. It is always my challenge to speak to my students in the right way so that they will listen.

Girls can be this cruel. Most parents have to deal with anger and tears at home about these situations. Counselors, administrators, and teachers at school try to give guidance and ask girls to treat each other better. In a sense, they are all vying for a new pecking order. They want to be in the popular group. Often, friendships change from one grade to another, and sometimes girls form fast friendships for many years to come. Parents need to understand why some friendships develop. For example,

Terry and Lois found each other in seventh grade. They both had mothers who drank too much and the girls both had strong personalities. They were left home alone a lot also. They had never told anyone else, but they were both sexually assaulted at an earlier age. Everyone in school knew how close they were—they were always together, and, when they could, they would try to get out of class and meet in the bathroom. They had a lot in common, and their friendship lasted for years.

In sixth grade, girls often want to do well academically, as they do in elementary school. The American Association of University Women has conducted research that reveals by eighth grade many girls do not want to get really high grades because they are more interested in boyfriends, and they do not want to appear "too smart." Thus, girls are at risk at the end of middle school of having declining grades. Many girls in eighth grade become obsessed with having a boyfriend. Another reason that their grades can decline is that they spend too much of their time thinking about and talking about having a boyfriend. They think that a boy likes them, but they're not sure. Parents need to understand the impact of this obsession. For example,

Laura appeared in my office one morning. She liked a certain boy and was not sure whether he liked her. Her friend Jane asked the boy, and he said that he did like Laura, but Johnny, another friend, said that wasn't true. Laura didn't know what to think or do. I suggested that she just be friendly to the boy to see where things led. We spent a long time talking about boy/girl relationships and what to expect. I wanted girls to understand that although they were very interested in finding out how serious a boy was about them, the boys were much more fickle and often didn't have a strong opinion about going out with them.

In addition, girls are bombarded in our society by sexual images. They're everywhere: on television, in movies, on cable, in magazines. The message given is that a girl must be pretty, thin, and wear provocative clothing. A girl wants to look good, to be popular, and to have a boyfriend. She sees skinny females in tight clothing in the media. She watches shows that seem to revolve around sexual relationships. This is a time when many girls lose their identity. They used to be interested in art or dancing, but now they only want to fulfill the American image of being beautiful.

When she was in elementary school, Catherine loved horses. Her parents provided her with private lessons and devoted a lot of time to enable her to fulfill her interest. By seventh grade, Catherine did not want to waste time with horseback riding. She was on the phone incessantly, and she fought with her mother over wearing tight tops. When her mother tried to talk to her, Catherine would yell at her and run to her room. What happened to my sweet daughter? her mother wondered.

When these changes in girls become extreme, they may be at great risk for developing eating disorders or depression. Both of these problems are very complex, and it is important for parents to be very alert in order to identify them early and seek intervention. Girls who develop eating disorders are often perfectionists, and they may have controlling parents. The girls focus on food, much as an addict focuses on drugs. A full-blown eating disorder requires a team of professionals: a medical doctor, a nutritionist, and a counselor. Food becomes an obsession, and denial and subterfuge are the game. A girl's friends know what is going on, but they often do not want to intervene. Girls with eating disorders will wear baggy clothes so that people do not notice that they are losing weight. As illogical as it may seem, a girl who is anorexic and weighs perhaps eighty pounds thinks she is fat. She sees herself as fat in the mirror even though the rest of the world sees skinny. It can be difficult for parents to detect the difference between a girl's desire to be thin and, therefore, her monitoring of what she eats, and the beginning of anorexia, or self-starvation, or bulimia, where a girl will binge on food and then make herself throw up.

If you have a young adolescent daughter, it is important to talk to her about her body. Does she feel pressure to lose weight? Does she compare herself with the music and movie stars who are unnaturally thin? Does she understand that we all inherit a body type with which we have to become comfortable? You can pretty much assume that most girls are concerned about their body image.

John, Mark, and David came to see me. These were eighth-grade boys who were popular. They were concerned about Jessica. They said that she was not eating at school, and another girl had told them that she had thrown up in the bathroom. They knew enough to know that this was serious, and they wanted me to talk to her. I knew that this would be difficult because if Jessica was developing an eating disorder she would certainly not want to tell me. In addition, I would have to call her mother because this was a situation involving danger to the child, and Jessica would be very angry at me for doing that. When a girl is caught with an eating disorder, she becomes very angry with the people who report her. This would be a difficult meeting.

Again, eighth grade marks the beginning of a vulnerable period for developing serious problems. Parents need to be aware of the signs of possible depression. These include loss of interest in normal activities, change in eating or sleeping habits, aggressive or acting-out behaviors, changes in relationships with others, a long-term change in mood or mood swings, and engaging in self-defeating behaviors (Gerald D. Oster and Sarah S. Montgomery, 1994). Parents should take any threat of suicide very seriously and seek help immediately. Temporary hospitalization may be necessary to protect a child. Precipitating signs of impending suicide attempts include giving away prized possessions, losing someone in death, having a family crisis, and facing the breakup of a romantic relationship.

Kathy came to me crying. She was very upset because her boyfriend just broke up with her. She said that she told something to her friend Jamie in first period, and Jamie said not to say it again. I knew what would follow. When I asked her what she had said, she said that she saw no reason to live. When I told her that I would have to call her mom because I was worried about her endangering her life, she said that she didn't mean it and that she would hate me if I called her mom. Luckily, one of her teachers happened to walk by my office, and I asked Kathy if it would be OK if she joined us. It was easier for me to minimize Kathy's anger if I had another adult to work with. As it turned out, Kathy's mother was grateful for the call. She came to school immediately, and we had a good discussion about Kathy's boyfriend plus other family problems. She promised to get counseling for Kathy.

Parents should seek help immediately because both eating disorders and depression can lead to extremely serious consequences. Eating disorders can be very difficult to cure once they are fully entrenched, and depression can lead to suicide. In the United States, the suicide rate of children ages ten to nineteen has increased for the past two decades. Suicide is associated with depression and with bipolar disorder, or manic depression, and the risk is increased when these disorders are combined with drug and alcohol use. Suicide is considered to be a major danger among adolescents. Medication and counseling can help to prevent suicide as well as help to solve problems causing depression.

Girls who feel unloved because of their family problems will often seek a boyfriend early. In families where there are no fathers, for whatever reasons, girls also are likely to seek a boyfriend. Absent fathers also increase a girl's vulnerability to developing an eating disorder or depression. These girls will take sexual risks early in order to feel loved. It is very important for the families of girls at risk to use preventive measures early in middle school. Prevention includes encouraging a girl to continue in her interests or hobbies and watching who her new friends are. Girls need to be educated about the influence of sexual messages that they see. Girls need to have definite goals for their future. They also need to understand that boys are more interested in temporary relationships and in sex, and that this will not fulfill their female needs but instead could cause them to become depressed when a boy's interest is short-lived.

When Alice, an eighth grader, broke up with her fifth boyfriend, she was devastated. She had had sex with all five in hopes of keeping them, and all five of them had lost interest in her. She was contemplating suicide. After she told her friend Tammy, Tammy told me about the suicide threat. I immediately called Alice's mother, who had to come to school because suicide threats are always taken seriously. I asked Alice and her mother to go to the local crisis center, and I recommended therapy. I also promised to have several discussions with Alice. Fortunately, Alice's mother recognized the seriousness of the problem, and Alice started private counseling. By the end of the eighth grade, she was much more confident. Unfortunately, I have had several girls whose mothers did not provide counseling, and those girls usually would continue to have sex with other boys, and I worried about them entering high school. And every year I have several suicide threats. It is always very frightening to me.

Thus, the transition from girl to woman that occurs in middle school is fraught with problems. Girls often have conflicts with their mothers at this age because their mothers are trying to protect them, and the girls want to make their own decisions. There are some rules that should stay rules, and there are others where mothers need to work on compromises with their daughters. The academic focus must always be present. Parents must try to get girls to see things in proper perspective, using humor and picking their battles so that the most important values remain honored. Children at this age have a difficult time seeing the future because it is so far away. Parents need to be constantly aware of what their children are doing so that the future can be bright.

Chapter 5

The Power of the Peer Group:
Clothes, Bullies, Drugs

Years ago children had many hours in a day when they would entertain themselves at home or, perhaps, play with one or two other children in the neighborhood. Today, life is very different. Children are being placed in groups with other children on a regular basis from the age of two, or earlier. Often they have no choice. Children with working parents may be enrolled in day care at a very early age, while children with a stay-at-home mother are often put into nursery schools for three to six hours a day at the age of two or three. It is rare that a preschool child just stays home today.

Now youngsters congregate in groups: day care groups, nursery school groups, play groups, after-school groups, sports groups, and other various activity groups. What is the effect on children of spending so many hours a day in groups? Often, the peer group has gained more power over a child than the parents have. Whoever spends the most time with a child may wield more influence.

When children get to middle school, they want to be accepted and they want to be popular. Think about clothes, for example. The power of advertising in the media has made certain kinds of clothes popular among children. Preoccupation with clothes is not a new phenomenon. However, today's preferences can include extremely expensive athletic shoes and jeans. Many parents cannot afford such prices for children's clothes. But the peer group can be so critical about clothing that a parent will recognize that the expenditure has to be made to keep peace in the family.

Jennifer came to my office crying. She had just gotten a new pair of fancy athletic shoes, and Diane, the most popular girl in the class, was angry at Jennifer because Diane wanted to get the shoes first. This may seem very silly, but I knew that this problem had to be settled. I called in Diane, and we held a conflict resolution session, where each girl had the opportunity to express her feelings to the other. Finally, both girls decided to wear the shoes the next day and walk down the hall together. When I intervened, the girls would usually become reasonable. I was very grateful for their cooperation.

The media in our society has become a central focus of children from middle school or earlier on up. They are all exposed to images on television, in movies, and in teen magazines, which set the standard for clothing and appearance. In recent years, very tight-fitting tops that accentuate a girl's breasts are popular. If all of the other girls have these tops, a parent will have to put up a strong fight to keep his or her daughter from wearing this fashion.

Mrs. McAllen called me, and I could tell that she was very concerned. Her daughter, Cindy, was in seventh grade. They had gone shopping the day before, and Cindy insisted on getting the new tank tops. Mrs. McAllen thought that they were all cut too low, and her daughter and she had an argument in the store. They ended up leaving with no purchases and no agreement. What should she do? Mrs. McAllen asked. I reminded her that she had to take a firm stand and explain her reasons. She should speak from her point of view, how she didn't want boys to think that Cindy was "easy," that fighting inappropriate fashion was difficult, but it was her job as a mother. It would be a lot easier if she could get other mothers to join her in the crusade.

Entire families in America used to live in the same cities. Most children had grandparents, aunts, and uncles to help raise them. Today, we are a mobile society, and the extended family is often absent. Who replaces the extended family? The peer group. Thus, parents are having a much more difficult time exerting a strong influence over the lives of their children.

Mrs. Kay called me to ask if I thought it was all right for her daughter to wear pantyhose in the sixth grade, as some of her friends were doing. Mrs. Kay had difficulty making a decision like this on her own. I said that I would look around at the girls and see whether they were wearing pantyhose, and I would call her back. The girls were, in fact, wearing them. I also asked one of the teachers who had a daughter in middle school, and she felt that pantyhose were proper to wear. I always value input from teachers about my students and their issues.

Children learn that an emotional tirade can wear down parents, so they will use that tactic whenever possible in order to be accepted by the peer group. Many parents are tired from their busy lives, and they give in to their children. Because of this, there can be a "Lord of the Flies" syndrome, where the peer group gives so much power to children that parents can be overruled.

We all watched Katie and Kim on a daily basis. They wore short skirts and revealing tops. We knew that they were best of friends, and often they would bring clothes to school to exchange. In addition, the girls were not motivated to do well in school, which resulted in average or low grades. When we had parent conferences about academic issues, the parents were often weak and unwilling to use strategies for change. It seemed that Katie and Kim were allowed to make most of the decisions in their lives. We knew who ruled those homes: it wasn't the parents!

A major problem—teasing—can develop from having too much social power. There have always been school bullies, but now there is teasing on a regular basis in school. One cause of this is television. Many comedy shows get their laughs from insults that the characters fire at each other. Children who watch a lot of television develop the use of insults as a form of social behavior. When a child who is sensitive reveals his or her hurt from teasing, a real problem can develop. If others add to the teasing in groups, a day can become unbearable for a child.

Nearly one-third of American children and teens report that they have experienced bullying, either as a target or as a perpetrator, according to an article in the April 25, 2001, issue of *The Journal of the American Medical Association*. The article defines bullying as a specific type of aggression in which the behavior is intended to harm or disturb, the behavior occurs repeatedly over time, and there is an imbalance of power, with a more powerful person or group attacking a less powerful one. The behavior may be physical, such as pushing and hitting, or verbal, such as name-calling, spreading rumors, shunning, or ridiculing. This behavior takes a psychological toll on the victim, and it also has a negative effect on the bully.

Victims may suffer from psychosomatic complaints, such as headaches and stomachaches, on a regular basis, and they may miss more school because the physical ailments give them an excuse to stay home, away from the bullies. Additionally, they may have troubled relationships with classmates, and they may feel very lonely. They may develop anxiety and depression to the extent that they need counseling. Furthermore, they often have low self-esteem because they feel powerless. If they do not get counseling to teach them to deal effectively with bullies, they may develop a "victim mentality" for much of their lives. This means that they may become passive in relationships and become easily controlled by others as adults. They do not solve problems effectively, and they blame life's problems on others (Dorothea M. Ross, 1996).

The bully also suffers from his or her behavior. Bullies have higher rates of alcohol and tobacco use and more negative attitudes toward school, but most report no difficulty in making friends. That is because physical aggression often brings power to people. Bullies may become more involved in antisocial behavior, which can bring them many problems in their adult lives. A high percentage of bullies end up with a criminal conviction in their early twenties.

Understanding how to respond to a bully in an effective manner is extremely important, especially in middle school, which has a higher frequency of bullying. A bully is always looking for a payoff: hurt feelings. The immediate reaction that a child gives to teasing sets him or her up for more or less teasing. If the child reveals through nonverbal behavior, such as frowning and cowering, that he or she is hurt, then the bully knows that this child is an easy target. Bullies often look for a physical characteristic to tease.

Mrs. Gordon called me because her son Harry was teased about being fat. I said that I would talk to Harry about his reaction to this taunt. The best reaction is either to ignore or to agree with the teaser. Without the payoff of hurt feelings, the teaser will go elsewhere. I knew that it would take a while for me to train Harry not to react. I planned to do some role-playing with him, and I suggested that his parents do the same.

The best course of action for victims involves several options. If a child can ignore the bully and honestly not care, the bully will know this. A second step is to agree with the bully and even try to become friends by using humor. "I know that I'm fat. I'm trying to exercise more to lose weight. Maybe in gym we could jog together, and you could tell me to keep going when I want to stop." It is also important for children to tell adults about bullying. Children are often afraid to tell their parents that they are being taunted because they are ashamed. Parents need to look for signs of problems, such as a decline in grades and an increase in health problems. A child who does not want to go to school has a serious problem. Parents need to alert the school about this problem and find professional counseling. There are anti-bullying curricula that some schools are implementing in an effort to reduce bullying. Bullying should be discussed in schools, and there should be clear rules against it. If there are no consequences, then the behavior will continue. All children need to be taught positive interpersonal skills.

The peer group takes on dangerous power when drugs, alcohol, and sex are involved. In fact, it is the need to fit in that causes early adolescents to begin to experiment with dangerous behaviors. They want to be accepted, and they do not want to be made fun of. So they may try risky behaviors when there is no adult present. In fact, the only way parents can hope to prevent experimentation with drugs is to talk frequently about the harm that drugs can cause.

I couldn't believe the commotion that day. Shirley, an eighth grader, had brought gelatin squares into the girls' bathroom in the morning. When it was discovered, the girls ran from the bathroom, and at first we didn't know what had happened. Then someone told us about "gelatin shooters." These are gelatin squares with vodka in them. The administration spent a long time investigating this one, and eventually Shirley was suspended for a week. Many of us had not heard of this method of alcohol use. We discovered that it is popular in college as a fast way of getting drunk. Often, it feels as though we are losing ground on protecting children.

And drugs can cause terrible harm. Seventh and eighth graders in suburban neighborhoods have access to alcohol and drugs. Most eighth graders know from whom they can purchase drugs. When parents go out of town, teenagers often use the occasion to have parties at their houses. Sometimes parties are crashed, and dangerous fighting can occur. The use of drugs and alcohol at parties can lead to date rape. Some drugs today can cause a girl to slip into unconsciousness, making her easy prey for a rapist. These drugs also can damage her brain.

Parents also should be aware of the use of inhalants today. These are chemicals that are found in common products that, when sniffed, produce a high. The problem with inhalants is that they are everywhere: in white correction fluid, magic markers, household products, gasoline, cleaners, and other products. Inhalants are extremely dangerous! In fact, there have been cases where children have died because they inhaled an extremely toxic substance quite rapidly. A parent should be alerted if a child asks for bottles of white correction fluid on a frequent basis.

When an adolescent becomes addicted to drugs, the family becomes engulfed in a horrible nightmare. The theory of addiction is that some people are vulnerable because of differences in the brain. There is an area of the brain that contains instincts and emotions. In people who do not become addicted, there are "high" brain waves that enable the person to feel good most of the time. In people who become addicted, those brain waves are low, resulting in a feeling of boredom and dissatisfaction much of the time. When a person drinks alcohol, the brain waves suddenly become high, making the person feel better. That section of the brain then slowly begins to negate the rational part of the person's brain, seeking to feel better with more alcohol and drugs.

Thus begins a life of lying, stealing, falling grades, and association with others who also are becoming addicted. Then begins a long period of denial by both the child and the parents. Parents will rationalize and hide from the truth. The child will develop a life that is controlled by the need to take drugs and alcohol, and he or she will also rationalize that quitting can occur whenever he or she wants. By the time parents discover that their child is addicted, the child is so irrational that the home becomes a terrible scene of fighting and misery.

Parents need to be extremely vigilant and knowledgeable about signs of addiction. Smoking is considered to be a gateway drug because it can lead to marijuana use. Marijuana today is much stronger than it was in decades past. It attaches itself to receptors in the brain, can be addictive, and can cause permanent damage to short-term memory of regular users. The harm that it does is gradual in nature. It distorts perceptions and causes a lack of motivation. Parents need to be alert to signs of possible marijuana use. Grades and attendance at school always decline in adolescents who are addicted. There is a loss of interest in outside activities and there can be isolation from the family, temper tantrums, and violence. After the first use of marijuana, experimentation can quickly develop into regular use. Unfortunately, parents may be in denial because they feel that they are losing their children and don't want to come down harshly on them. Parents may tell themselves that this is just a stage, that other kids force their child to experiment, and that their kids are honest with them: this sort of thinking is self-deception.

By the time a parent seeks a solution for a teen who is addicted, there still will be a long road to recovery even if the teen is willing to cooperate. This can take many years and devastate the family.

Eddie and Stan were the best of friends in sixth and seventh grades. Then, Stan began to drink and smoke marijuana in eighth grade. Eddie wasn't interested. Stan's dad had a problem with alcohol. By tenth grade, Stan had missed much school, and he had a full-blown addiction. He dropped out of school and eventually ended up in a special school. Eddie saw him several years later and was surprised by how much Stan had changed. His personality was different. It seemed very sad to Eddie.

The strongest force against peer pressure can come from the parents, who need to have continuing discussions with their children about the pressure they are experiencing and how they can manage it. Parents should discuss the meaning of true friendship so that adolescents can question a supposed friend who could lead them into trouble. Parents need to take the role of the "heavy" so that children can say that their parents will not allow them to be alone in homes. The dangers adolescents face are so serious that they can have long-lasting, devastating effects. Parents must take a strong stance and communicate often with their children in order to keep them on the right track.

Chapter 6

School Achievement

Middle school, again, is another period of huge adjustment, this time to academic expectations. The focus of elementary school is to learn reading, writing, and mathematics, and to develop self-esteem through this accomplishment. Elementary teachers are supposed to give high grades and write positive comments on report cards so that children are not discouraged from the learning process. The only hint that there might be a problem with achievement is a comment such as, "Kevin needs to try harder."

Middle school is an entirely different challenge. Now there are seven periods, and four or five different academic teachers daily. Or, there could be block scheduling, where students have longer periods but they do not have every subject every day. Students are expected to listen well, write down homework assignments, remember to bring all necessary books and materials to each separate class, bring all materials home, do homework, organize it, and return it the next day. And tests now involve studying, which many students do not know how to do. If you review material in an elementary class before a test, you are not studying. Studying requires organizing, understanding, and repeating material at home.

This is a formidable task for sixth graders. Seventh graders begin to understand the demands made on them. Eighth graders really don't want to spend a lot of time on academics because social issues are more important, and they feel that nothing else counts until high school. This is an area where middle school is really a middle child.

Parents need to know this important fact: just because your child is looking older does not mean that he or she has the skills or maturity to do what is expected academically to be successful in middle school. Parents should monitor schoolwork on a daily basis. They must be aware of assignments and tests and help their children to organize all work before they go to bed. Parents should take everything out of the book bag each night with their children and discuss the class assignments.

I was always surprised when I had to call a parent about an academic problem, and the parent said that they thought that their child could be more independent now that he or she was in middle school. I knew that just the opposite was true. I had to remind parents to be involved with their children's schoolwork. It seems today that many parents would like to have *less* responsibility for this once their children leave elementary school, but they should assume even *more* responsibility. In middle school, I would explain, there are more teachers to adjust to, and the classes become more difficult.

What continues to amaze teachers in middle school is that parents say they saw the homework being done the night before, but the child cannot find it the next day to give to the teacher. There is also an enormous problem with knowing exactly what the homework is. Some middle schools have adopted two specific strategies to address that problem. First, many schools have an assignment or agenda book, which is a notebook-sized calendar with spaces to write down assignments daily. Second, many schools have a homework hotline number where teachers phone in the night's assignment, hoping that parents will call in order to verify what is written in the assignment book. Additionally, the assignment book can be signed by the teacher to verify the correctness of what the child writes. There are also daily progress reports where the teacher can circle whether or not the homework was handed in.

Parents should devise appropriate rewards (these work better) or consequences. When parents follow through consistently and check on homework, academic success is more easily achieved. Parents should work with the counselor in processing these daily or weekly reports. Students should have the responsibility of bringing the forms to the teachers and retrieving them (see Figures 6.1, 6.2, 6.3, and 6.4).

Even with these strategies, getting homework completed is a major problem. The reason is that the word "home" is in homework, meaning that parents need to take the time each night to be sure that homework is done. Many parents are tired from work and have domestic duties to do, so they let homework slack. But if parents do not get involved on a nightly basis, the percentage of homework that is done will drop. Parents should make doing homework just as important as eating dinner. The curriculum in many schools is so extensive that all learning cannot be

Figure 6.1
Example of a Successful Behavior Log

Name: _____

Teacher: _____

Week of: _____   Please mark in each box. G = Good, S = Satisfactory, S— =Unsatisfactory

	Listened and followed directions	Was a quiet worker	Stayed in my seat	Completed all my classwork	Returned my homework	Showed respect for myself and others/Teacher	Your initials please
MONDAY							
TUESDAY							
WEDNESDAY							
THURSDAY							
FRIDAY							

Figure 6.2
Another Example of a Behavior Log

Name _____   Date _____
Please comment if there is a problem.

1.	Tests/quizzes	Good	Satisfactory	Problem
2.	Homework	Good	Satisfactory	Problem
3.	Following Directions	Good	Satisfactory	Problem
4.	Getting Along with Peers	Good	Satisfactory	Problem
5.	Working Independently	Good	Satisfactory	Problem
6.	Getting Along with Adults	Good	Satisfactory	Problem
7.	Working in Groups	Good	Satisfactory	Problem
8.	Paying Attention	Good	Satisfactory	Problem
9.	Respecting Rules	Good	Satisfactory	Problem
10.	Motivation	Good	Satisfactory	Problem
11.	Accepting Criticism	Good	Satisfactory	Problem
12.	Giving Criticism	Good	Satisfactory	Problem
13.	Mature Behavior	Good	Satisfactory	Problem

done during the school day. Even though children will protest, parents should be involved.

Mrs. Wilson could not figure out how to get her son to do homework each night. I suggested that there be a period of one and one-half hours each night when the entire house would be quiet, and everyone in the house would be doing homework or reading. This daily habit could bring much success. Mrs. Wilson decided to try it.

I also suggest to parents that each child have a large calendar in the kitchen where all major assignments and tests can be written down. Parents should help children to organize large assignments into smaller chunks so that last-minute panic does not ensue. Children also need help every night in organizing their notebook and managing their time (see Figure 6.5).

Locker cleanout was always a pain to Mr. Henson, the building service supervisor. How could kids just jam handfuls of papers into their lockers and leave them there for weeks? Each hall required giant wastebaskets at cleanout time to

Figure 6.3
Example of a Daily Progress Report

NAME_____DATE_____

ENGLISH

1. Homework completed   Yes   No

2. Classwork completed   Yes   No

3. Materials brought to class   Yes   No

4. Appropriate behavior   Yes   No

Teacher's signature_____Comments_____

SCIENCE

1. Homework completed   Yes   No

2. Classwork completed   Yes   No

3. Materials brought to class   Yes   No

4. Appropriate behavior   Yes   No

Teacher's signature_____Comments_____

MATH

1. Homework completed   Yes   No

2. Classwork completed   Yes   No

3. Materials brought to class   Yes   No

4. Appropriate behavior   Yes   No

Teacher's signature_____Comments_____

SOCIAL STUDIES

1. Homework completed   Yes   No

2. Classwork completed   Yes   No

3. Materials brought to class   Yes   No

4. Appropriate behavior   Yes   No

Teacher's signature_____Comments_____

Figure 6.4
Example of a Weekly Progress Report

Weekly Progress Report of _____

(Student Name)

Week of _____

(Date)

Please evaluate the following characteristics using the three-point scale below:

1-very good   2-satisfactory   3-unsatisfactory

CLASSWORK	ENGLISH	WORLD STUDIES	MATH	SCIENCE
1. Effort				
2. Class participation				
3. Behavior				
4. Homework				
5. Grades earned for the week				
TEACHER'S INITIALS				

Comment to Parents: Please list missing work that can be made up.

_____

Parent's Signature

_____

Counselor's Signature

Figure 6.5
Time Management Grid

The student should fill in time for all activities, including the dinner hour. The student should then select three or four half-hour periods daily for homework and study. A break should occur after each half-hour period. When a schedule is made and the student is committed to it, success will come more easily.

Student: _____ From ___/___/___ to___/___/___

	M	T	W	TH	F
3:30-4:00					
4:00-4:30					
4:30-5:00					
5:00-5:30					
5:30-6:00					
6:00-6:30					
6:30-7:00					
7:00-7:30					
7:30-8:00					
8:00-8:30					
8:30-9:00					
9:00-9:30					
9:30-10:00					
10:00-10:30					
10:30-11:00					

accommodate the trash in all of the lockers. It was a rare locker that was organized. If we didn't have locker cleanouts every month, I don't know what would
happen. It seems that children don't want to take the time to think and organize.

A child's motivation to do well in school is primarily related to his or
her internal beliefs. If a child does not have a learning problem, these
are the possible negative beliefs that may cause underachievement:

"I have no control over what happens to me."

"If something is not perfect, it's awful."

"Growing up doesn't get you anywhere."

"I am incompetent and adults are not consistently reliable."

"My parents will fix anything for me. I don't have to be responsible."

"My parents are having problems and I want to take the focus off their problems
   by being a problem myself."

"My brothers/sisters are good students, so I will be a poor student."

"I am very angry about problems at home."

"There are too many emotions in my head and I can't concentrate."

Obviously, there are family and emotional problems here, and outside
professional intervention such as counseling would be necessary to make
positive change. No children want to get low report card grades. When
achievement is low, there is either a learning problem, such as attention
deficit disorder or a learning disability, or there are emotional and family
problems. Parents should be concerned and take an honest look at what
could be causing a problem in low achievement. If they don't, low
achievement may not change.

Personality characteristics and goals are influenced by parental expectations. If we tell our children of our expectations of positive behavior
and good grades on a regular basis, our children will try to fulfill those
expectations. If we help our children to set short- and long-term goals,
they will aim for them (see Figure 6.6). There are three parenting styles,
each of which can result in specific outcomes (Barbara Coloroso, 1995).
Authoritarian parents make rules without explanation and attempt to
control children in a harsh manner. This can result in rebelliousness and
a tendency to manipulate in children. Permissive parents do not give
children boundaries and self-control. These children often have difficulty
forming positive work habits. However, the best style of parenting is
authoritative yet democratic, where the parents are the leaders, but they
allow children to discuss rules, ideas, and plans. The parents are role
models of compromise and empathy, which are important qualities for
children to learn.

Too many parents do not understand that when a child has a problem

Figure 6.6
Goal Sheet

Name: _____   Date: _____

HOW I PLAN TO IMPROVE MY SCHOOL PERFORMANCE

WHAT I NEED TO DO	HOW I PLAN TO DO IT	WHEN I PLAN TO DO IT

in achievement, punishment does not really help. Grounding a child and taking away privileges do not teach study and organization skills. They only create animosity in children, which does not influence them to be better students.

I received another phone call from a parent who was concerned about Ds on her child's report card. The parent had told her child that he was grounded for two weeks. I suggested a more positive plan. Each night the child would sit at the dining room table and do homework, study, or read a book. Studying should be done in increments of twenty minutes with a five-minute break, and a total of two hours should be devoted to this. Meanwhile, mom could read a book, and the house should be quiet. In addition, the child had to be required to write down the daily assignments. The parents could use a contract with rewards to try to change the child's behavior (see Figure 6.7).

School grades are comprised of daily grades. Therefore, daily time allotted to school contributes to good grades. When the evening study time in the house is combined with daily progress reports and signed assignment books, good grades usually ensue. Rewards always work better than punishments once children leave elementary school.

Another way to effect achievement is to analyze the learning style of a specific student and provide supports when necessary. There are three learning styles: auditory, visual, and haptic (hands-on) (Lynn O'Brien, 1990), and there are learning styles assessments available that can reveal a learner's strengths. Auditory learners learn better by listening. Studying aloud with a friend and making tapes of information can be helpful. Visual learners learn better by watching. These students need to take notes, write things down, and study by themselves. Finally, haptic learn.-ers need to use their bodies when studying, perhaps by walking around or moving around on the floor.

The new social studies teacher often tried to incorporate in his lessons the three learning channels. When he had to lecture, he would use the overhead projector so that students could see and hear at the same time, and he tried to add physical projects to assignments so that students could use different skills to enhance their grades. He knew that he had to do this to reach all of his students and give them an opportunity to succeed on different levels.

Another way parents can better understand their children's learning style is with the theory of multiple intelligences (Howard Gardner, 2000). Most learning in school involves verbal and mathematical ability. But there are other intelligences that humans have, including musical, bodily, spatial, interpersonal, and intra-personal. What this means is that someone can be very talented in art but have difficulty writing lengthy paragraphs. Many schools are now recognizing the theory of multiple

Figure 6.7
Example of a Parent/Child Contract

I. RESPONSIBILITIES OF THE CHILD
    1. Will complete each homework assignment on time.
    2. After being absent, will obtain missed work and turn it in on time.
    3. Will accurately record each homework assignment in his assignment book daily.
    4. Will have daily progress report completed and signed by each teacher.
    5. After school, will take a break and then begin homework by 4 P.M., starting with the hardest subjects.

II. REWARDS GIVEN BY THE PARENT
    1. For successful completion of the above, each week you will select one of the following:
        a. Attend a movie of his or her choice.
        b. Rent two movies.
        c. Go out to dinner at a place of his or her choosing.
        d. Receive $5.00.
    2. For successful completion of the above for three of every four weeks, pick one of the following:
        a. Receive $10.00.
        b. Buy a nonviolent Playstation game of your choosing, paying half.
        c. Go to the batting cage.
        d. Take a friend to the movie.
        e. Have Dad make his or her bed for a week.

III. PENALTIES
    1. For each week that you do not complete any of the responsibilities, you will do the following at Mom and Dad's choice:
        a. Not play any video games for one day, or
        b. No roller blading for one day, or
        c. No television for one day, or
        d. Perform extra home chores for significant failure four or more times of items one through five during any one week. For example, dusting, cleaning up the basement play area, cleaning the bathroom, etc.

THIS CONTRACT CAN BE REWRITTEN AT ANY TIME.

Signatures: _____

intelligences, and teachers try to infuse those intelligences into the academic curricula. For example, a project on World War II can bring in the role of music, costumes, and movements in the German military showing how they helped to mesmerize the German public.

Thus, parents and teachers must analyze school achievement from many areas. There is usually not a simple analysis to explain underachievement. What is important is for a child to know that parents and school will always work together to enable a child to be as successful as possible.

Chapter 7

How to Communicate with Teachers

When your child enters middle school, you should understand that the teacher/parent relationship will be different from that in elementary school. In elementary school, you had a primary teacher to communicate with each year. You could depend on phone calls from that teacher who knew your child fairly well.

The situation is different in middle school. It is important for you to appreciate this difference so that you can maintain good communication about your child's progress. It is also important that you understand that your child has several groups of teachers and that you may have to make phone calls to individuals from each group.

Most middle schools are made up of academic teams. These include the teachers of English, math, science, social studies, and, possibly, reading. These teams are located near each other, and they meet regularly to discuss student needs. There is also an arts department, including art, music, technical education, home economics, among others; a foreign language department, which usually teaches seventh and eighth graders; a physical education department; and, finally, administration and counseling departments. These groups of people do not meet together on a regular basis to discuss students unless they are individually involved in a parent conference. So, if you have a concern about any of these areas, call the individual teacher, and, of course, the counselor, to get information and to help your child.

Before you start talking to teachers, I suggest that you consider the complexity of a teacher's day so that you will understand how your questions and concerns fit into his or her schedule. For each class, teachers must prepare lessons, change activities within a class period, and anticipate problems in understanding or completing the lessons. Teachers must meet objectives, and they are under constant pressure to help their students to do well on standardized tests. So, their first concern is planning effective and interesting lessons for the day, and they may teach two or three levels of classes or subjects.

Within the learning environment, teachers must be constantly aware of student needs and behavior. Students in middle school need lots of help with organization. Most teachers use a variety of strategies to teach organizational skills and to help students organize their thinking. Teachers must also be aware of individual student needs, including monitoring accommodations stated on 504 plans and Individual Educational Plans (IEP). There are students who have needs that have not been identified. And then there are social and emotional needs and problems that teachers have to manage on a continual basis. Some students don't do homework. Others are eager to learn.

A teacher's day also includes conferring with colleagues and administration and returning parent phone calls. Teachers have to copy materials for class and attend meetings. Then, they end their day by grading tests and projects. Each one of these tasks can include checking more than 150 papers. While teachers are very busy and often feel rushed, they want to be in a partnership with you so that your child can be successful. They are well aware that parents are key to student achievement.

When you communicate with teachers, let them know that you want to work with them to help your child. Don't be confrontational or accusatory. Remember that there are always at least two sides to every story.

Mrs. Ridge called me and she was quite angry. Her son, Jerry, told her last night that he left his math homework paper in his sixth-period classroom. When he went to retrieve it, Mrs. Gillingham, his teacher, wouldn't let him come into the room to look for it, and so he didn't do the math homework. Mrs. Ridge was a strict parent who monitored homework carefully. I told her that I would have to ask the teacher what happened. The story was a typical middle school experience. Mrs. Gillingham said that Jerry had come back for the paper. He did find it and ran down the hall with it, and then another boy grabbed it from his hand, and it ripped. Jerry, who told me that this was true, was embarrassed to take it home for fear that his mother would get angry because the paper was ripped. I explained to Jerry that he could have gone to his math teacher to get another paper, or Mrs. Gillingham could have written him a note to give to his mother. I also suggested to Mrs. Ridge that she tell Jerry that she would not get angry at him for something like this. When a parent is patient, a child feels more comfortable about explaining a problem.

Teachers focus on what is working and what is not. They have to be aware of problems, and they would like your help in solving them. When you attend a teacher/parent conference, you may notice that teachers focus on the negative. It is not that teachers are negative people, it's just that negative behaviors in class, whether acting out, not paying attention, or not doing work, interfere with learning for all of the students, as well as the one causing the trouble. So, teachers are looking at such problems to find solutions. Please do not interpret this as a dislike for your child. Be a willing partner in helping your child to change behaviors. Some problems are long-term and have not been diagnosed, and others are adjustment problems. Both parent and teacher must give students the message that school is important, that they can do the work, and that the adults will not give up on them.

Janet, a sixth grader, had problems writing paragraphs. She had come in for extra help after school, but she was still struggling. Her teacher began to suspect a learning disability, which often is revealed when a student is having difficulty with the writing process. We began with a parent conference. The English teacher showed Janet's mom how she could help her at home to organize her ideas first. We decided to go to a screening Individual Education Plan meeting to investigate possible learning disabilities because other teachers saw the same problem. But we gave Janet the message that we believed that with extra help she could be successful. We would never give up on her, and we did not want her to give up trying!

When you go to a conference, bring a pen and paper to take notes or jot down ideas, even though you should receive notes from a meeting. Ask for elaboration on your child's strengths. Ask for positive comments so that everyone can have a balanced view. Also ask teachers to gather work samples for you. Ask lots of questions. Probe to get specific details about problems. If the problem is homework, ask when and where each teacher posts daily homework so that your child can see it. It may not be the same in each class. Which homework assignments were not done, and should you monitor homework nightly? Is there a lack of understanding or a lack of will? If the problem involves tests, look at what kinds of learning are required. Does the problem deal with memorizing, writing, explaining terms, understanding concepts, applying information, and so forth?

Find out the areas in which your child needs help and where there are weaknesses in learning. Can the student strengthen these areas on his or her own? Should you help your child to review? If the problem is organization, what system does the teacher use? What does the notebook look like? Does the teacher ask for additional folders? Should you help your child organize papers nightly? Should you go through the backpack with your child each weekend?

There also may be questions to ask about social difficulties. If the problem is participation, ask if your child is shy or unprepared. Is there a social problem with another student that prevents your child from participating? If the problem is shyness, can your child volunteer once a day in each class to become more comfortable? If the problem is behavior, what is the exact behavior, and when and where does it occur? Is it aligned with the time of day or the style of the teacher or the subject? Can you and the teacher create a contract that monitors behavior either daily or weekly (see the sample forms in Chapter 6)? Rewarding your child for improved behavior can bring success.

Suzette had a problem of impulsively blurting out requests for help whenever she felt frustrated. This seemed to happen more often in math than in any other subject. She wanted to do well, but she often needed instructions repeated, and she wanted it done immediately! At a parent conference with the team, we asked her to try some strategies. We wanted her to know that we all believed that she could succeed. Then we suggested that she count to ten to herself to gain self-control. She could raise her hand but not speak until recognized. She could make a check mark next to the problem that was bothering her. If the teacher could not get to her in time, then she would agree to see her at lunch. We wanted her to feel that she would definitely get the help she needed to relieve her frustration. Then, privately, I spoke to her mother about conferring with the doctor if these strategies did not work. Perhaps there was an underlying condition, such as attention deficit disorder, or other possible problems.

Ask your child for his or her perception of problems. See if your child can identify possible problems and possible solutions. Let your child hear your positive expectations. Look for action steps and write them down. Do your part to help your child and keep communicating with the teachers. Meanwhile, always get feedback and plan for a follow-up conference to check for improvement. You can see that discussing your child's problems with teachers takes some understanding of how middle schools are organized, the kinds of problems that can occur, and knowledge of your child. With some preparation on your part, the parent/teacher conference can be very successful. When parents and teachers work together, a student will improve!

Chapter 8

Outside Interests and Positive Identity

It is very important that parents try to structure the life of a young adolescent to combat the negative forces of the peer group and the media. Basically, the more time a child has to associate only with the peer group, the less influence a parent has. The more time a child has to watch TV and movies and to be entertained by video systems, the less the child will develop a sense of his or her strengths and interests and abilities. These skills are crucial because they will lead a child to a future career.

Elementary school is a time when children start to become involved in organized sports and various hobbies and music and dance lessons. These are all beneficial for children as long as they also have free time to play with toys and to explore the world of nature. Children develop a sense of what they like to do and what they are good at. This is a time of early self-discovery that can contribute to the skills and interests that we maintain in adulthood.

In middle school, children start to move away from these interests because they would rather be with their peer group and socialize. They would rather go to the mall with friends and walk around. They like to hang out in groups and talk on the phone for hours. And they become interested in TV shows and movies that focus on teenagers and their relationships. These are all forces that work against a child's ability to develop his or her individual identity. Socializing, of course, is important because an early adolescent is starting to analyze who he or she is and to develop more sophisticated social skills. Children gradually grow away from their parents' influence, but in middle school, parents must be careful to keep everything balanced. And they must be mindful of the fact that kids in groups can get into trouble.

Mrs. Whalen called me and she was very upset. She allowed Bobby to go to the mall with his friends, and they were caught shoplifting. The entire family was turned upside down. Bobby had never been in trouble before. He said that it was Brian who did the shoplifting and he was just there. However, the police were called, and it was an ugly mess. I told Mrs. Whalen that from now on she would have to be sure that an adult was present when Bobby was with friends, not because she couldn't trust Bobby, but because she couldn't trust his friends. Children in groups become bold and may try behaviors that get them in trouble. Bobby would protest, but this was important for his protection. Middle school is not a time to stop watching your children.

However, as young adolescents move away from individual interests toward a desire to be in groups, their confidence erodes as they are exposed to the daily give and take of critical comments from their peers. Where does high self-esteem come from? It comes from doing things in a successful way. It comes from being good at sports and playing on a team. It comes from becoming a better musician and practicing daily. It also comes from doing homework and studying for tests and getting good grades. It comes from being responsible and being rewarded for that. It does not come from the peer group in middle school. In fact, the peer group is what causes much self-doubt among early adolescents because there are so many insults thrown about. This is why it is so important for parents to try to have their children maintain those earlier interests and hobbies, as well as to put in daily effort in schoolwork.

Mrs. Green called me because Sharon, her seventh grader, was having emotional fits at home. Sharon didn't want to be in band anymore, and she was sure that some girls in school did not like her. I discussed the fact that band can be a wonderful activity in high school that provides supervised time and skill development as well as social time with a good group of kids. I agreed to talk to Sharon about how much fun the band kids have in high school. As for some girls not liking her, the fickle nature of middle schoolers meant that friendships could change on a continual basis. I would talk to Sharon about this, too.

So here begins a push-pull between parents and preadolescents. Parents must continue to try to influence their children to keep up the activities and hobbies that they had in elementary school. Preadolescents need to be kept busy most of the time. For those who are athletic, participating in sports is a wonderful use of time with practices and games. Musical and artistic talent also can help a child to fill hours and keep up their interests. Hobbies and collections can continue to amuse a child. Of course, reading activities by the entire family can influence a child and help him or her to spend time wisely. If a daily reading time is established at an early age, it can continue throughout middle school and will have a positive effect on learning. After all, most learning requires reading. It is also a good idea to introduce volunteer activities at an early age.

Mrs. Jensen called me, and she was very excited. Shari and her friend Lori, both seventh graders, had decided to volunteer at the local nursing home. They were having a great time entertaining the residents, playing the piano and singing. They decided that they wanted to polish the nails of the ladies. I said that this was a superb activity, keeping the girls busy and teaching them to help other. This was a "good news" call!

Parents should make use of the community to enable these positive activities to continue to take place. Flexible work schedules and car-pooling can ensure that activities will continue. For young adolescents, the hours between 4:00 P.M. and 6:00 P.M. are a time when children can get into trouble and experiment with risky behaviors. It is important for parents to take advantage of after-school activities and to network and take turns having friends over where there is an adult present so that children will be monitored during those hours.

Everyone knew that Jack's parents would not be home until 7:00 each night. There was a small group of friends who also had parents who came home late. Their parents would call them to check up on them, but since they were in the same neighborhood, they still had plenty of time to go to Jack's to have a beer, which Jack's older brother bought for them. Some of them were really getting to like the taste of beer.

Parents who do not appreciate the dangers of unsupervised youngsters are in denial. The end result is a child who gets into serious trouble. Parents need to rearrange their lives when their children are in middle school so that they will be able to monitor them. At age twelve or thirteen, a child is old enough legally to be left alone, but to allow them to be unmonitored at this age is to invite trouble.

Chapter 9

The Sexual Messages in Our Society

Do you remember television, movies, and magazines of the 1950s? There were certain lines that were not crossed. For example, husbands and wives were shown in twin beds. Most romantic scenes involved just kissing, and references to having sex were rarely made. Consider what women wore. They had dresses with full skirts and, perhaps, a v-neckline. Marilyn Monroe's most famous picture showed her standing above a subway grate on a city sidewalk with air pushing up her dress. She was still basically covered, and she had a plunging neckline that revealed some of her curves. But did you know that Marilyn Monroe was a size 12? In those days, a perfect figure was considered to be 36–24–36. That was a well-shaped, but not a skinny, figure. Today, that size 12 dress is considered to be overweight in Hollywood, which has led to an obsession with being skinny among most adolescent girls. In addition, people were seen in relationships that centered around marriage and the family. Sex was not really a topic for television, and movies handled sex in a subtle way.

This has all changed dramatically. Today, television and movies seem to revolve around sex as well as violence. And to make matters worse, the teen population has been identified as increasing in numbers and in economic power, so more and more movies and shows are aimed at the teenage audience. Most of the television shows that are popular with teens today have female stars that dress in tight, revealing clothing and stress love relationships with discussions of sex.

Mrs. Harvey watched as her thirteen-year-old son surfed the channels with his remote. He stopped on a station where many older teens were at a beach. The girls wore bikini bathing suits, and the boys wore regular bathing suits. They were all dancing to popular music, and you could see the boys focusing on the girls' bodies. When Mrs. Harvey asked her son to change the station, he yelled back that the song they were playing was his favorite. She decided that she and his dad should talk to him about respecting girls and not just viewing them as sex objects. This would not be an easy conversation.

This is a rather common scene on television. And what about movies? Even though there are ratings, many preadolescents can get into whatever movies they want. Movies today reveal the same images: women dressed in a sexy manner and sexual relationships abounding.

What about teen magazines? The magazines that the girls are most interested in usually show females in provocative positions with sexy clothing. And what about clothing manufacturers? Short tops where the belly button is revealed have been popular for several years. This year, the popular style is a tank top either without a bra or with bra straps showing. And what do you think the effect of these revealing clothes has on boys? Combine that with kids talking about suggestive movies and TV shows, and you have both sexes thinking a lot about sex. Parents and teachers are concerned about this serious problem and are seeking answers. For example,

At the faculty meeting, several teachers brought up the topic of girls revealing too much skin in school. Boys also were wearing pants that were falling down, revealing their boxer shorts. Should the teachers say anything to the students about this? Would the parents object? What was the administration's viewpoint? Should students be sent to the office? Do you remember last year when we made girls who were wearing provocative tops put on tee shirts with the school's name on them? There were many questions that needed to be answered.

Mothers really suffer with this problem today. Girls want to be popular, and they love the latest fashion. Starting in young adolescence, girls also want to become more independent, and one way to do this is to fight with their mothers. So when their mothers take a strong stance about this issue because they worry about their daughters experimenting with sex at an early age, there is a lot of arguing in homes. And, the focus on skinny bodies has opened the door for the development of eating disorders in adolescent girls. There is probably not a girl who believes that her body is OK the way it is. In fact, there are very few women who feel that way. It is almost funny that in the 1800s in this country, extra weight was a sign of wealth because it proved that a family had money for food.

Mrs. Taylor called and pleaded with me to talk to her daughter about the tight tops that she wanted to wear. Mrs. Taylor thought that perhaps I would have more influence because I wasn't the mother. She was also worried about her daughter's obsession with food and she wanted to get some information about signs of an eating disorder. I had piles of material to share with Mrs. Taylor. Because I was particularly worried about the possibility of an eating disorder, I asked Mrs. Taylor to come to my office so I could explain the material that I would give her.

How can parents protect their girls and boys from the powerful influence of sexual messages in the media today? They must communicate with their children and stand firm with their beliefs and standards. Parents must talk to both girls and boys because the boys must learn to control their sexual urges and act responsibly. When talking to their children, parents must be careful to listen to their children's viewpoint. It is also important to stress that sexual experimentation today can result in sexually transmitted diseases, including AIDS. Teenagers tend to feel that they are invincible or that trying something once will not harm them. It is important for parents to illustrate what the word *risk* means in as many ways as possible.

Mrs. Montgomery decided to ask her daughter to do research on the Internet for sexually transmitted diseases, while Mrs. Montgomery watched. Her daughter was amazed at how many diseases there were, and that some of them had no immediate symptoms. Then, Mrs. Montgomery asked her daughter how many sex partners she wanted to have before she got married. They did the arithmetic to see what would happen if her daughter had sex with two boys a year. In ten years, that would be twenty sex partners. Is that what she wanted? asked the mom. And don't forget that those boys have multiple partners also. She asked her daughter what effect that might have on her.

Parents should talk often and openly to their children. Fathers should explain to their daughters that they will closely monitor their activities with boys, and they will let the boys know that. Mothers should tell their sons that girls should be treated with respect, just as they would want their mother treated. There are some counselors who are developing girls' discussion groups that look at teen magazines and the media and the messages that they give. Parents should look for these kinds of groups for their children to join. And parents should not be afraid to use the word "no," and they should explain their reasons for using that word.

It is also a good idea for parents to contact the parents of their children's friends. Get together and discuss these issues. Agreement with other parents on standards for behavior gives you extra power, much as relatives used to have when there were extended families living in the same city. If teens can have power in numbers, so can parents.

Chapter 10

Effective Communication

Here is the challenge for parents with children aged from about twelve into adolescence: parents must talk to them about drugs and sex, while bearing in mind that children do not want to be lectured because they would rather talk to their peers. Thus, it is imperative that parents develop positive communication skills with their teens.

Life is all about communication. As human beings we easily give way to anger and frustration. As thinking humans, we can temper our words and attitudes so that we can work effectively with our children. For every negative or critical statement that you make to your children, you should make five positive comments: 5 to 1. Think about it. As parents, we often correct and judge our children more than we realize. People always remember negative remarks made to them. Thus, we must balance the negative by making many positive comments (see Figure 10.1).

Helen asked her son to please clean up his dishes. He was watching TV, of course. It always took patience to get him to do something around the house. Even though she had to ask him three times, she knew that she needed to interject some pleasant conversation so that they could maintain a positive relationship. If she kept harping on the dishes, he would get angry, and then she would get angry. You certainly had to work hard at your relationship with your teen! she thought.

Expect young adolescents to be argumentative. Expect them to appear to be on edge and angry often. They are having a difficult time under-

Figure 10.1
Ways to Praise Children

Remember: There should be five positive comments for every negative comment given.

You're doing a super job.
You did a lot of work today.
That's really good.
You are really something.
You're doing a fine job.
I love you.
Nice going.
That's coming along nicely.
You look really good today.
You outdid yourself.
Terrific.
That's much better.
That was really nice of you.
Good for you.
Excellent.
Super job.
Thanks for helping.
That's a neat idea.
That's really nice.
Keep up the good work.

You're such a big help.
Good thinking.
Way to go.
Wonderful.
I knew you could do it.
You're doing beautifully.
You're very good at that.
I'm very proud of you.
That's really good.
You worked well today.
Thanks for remembering.
You've improved a lot.
You figured that out quickly.
Tremendous!
You're getting better and better.
How did you think of that?
It's so nice to be around you.
You're a great son (daughter).
You are so smart.
How did you figure that out?

standing themselves and the forces that are acting on them: peers have demands, schools have demands, and parents have demands. The one area where they can let out frustration safely is at home with their parents. They walk on eggshells with their peers, and they could get in trouble in school if they become angry. Home is the only safe place to vent.

To adolescents the process of arguing with their parents is more important than the end result. If they can keep parents arguing, teens can vent their frustrations and feel that they have some power in the communication process. Therefore, moms and dads should not allow themselves to become engaged in long arguments. It is good to listen and to work for a compromise, but once a parent makes a decision, that should be the end of the conversation. Teens also will try to use emotions to influence their parents. They know that parents get upset with temper outbursts, and that sometimes parents will give in at that point. Do not allow your child's temper to influence your decisions. If you are both very angry, make a decision later. Or, write a note to your child where

Figure 10.2
Blank Letter: Write about a Problem You Are Having

—————————————
DATE

Dear_____.

—————————————————————————————
—————————————————————————————
—————————————————————————————
—————————————————————————————
—————————————————————————————
—————————————————————————————
—————————————————————————————
—————————————————————————————
—————————————————————————————
—————————————————————————————
—————————————————————————————
—————————————————————————————
—————————————————————————————
—————————————————————————————
—————————————————————————————
—————————————————————————————
—————————————————————————————

                                   —————————————,

                                   —————————————

you briefly explain a problem, express your feelings, and recommend a solution (see Figure 10.2). Then talk later when tempers cool.

Brian wanted to extend his curfew for Friday night. He knew that if he got very angry, his parents would give in. When he tried this strategy again and it did not work, he didn't know what to do to get his way. He tried getting angrier, but his parents didn't give in. He was forced to compromise. His parents felt as if they had regained some measure of control. They hoped that it would last for a while.

There are many positive communication strategies—active listening is one of them (Marlene Brusko, 1986). Active listening occurs when you mirror another person's feelings so that he or she feels understood. When a person feels understood, the doors to further communication open. In fact, you are listening for the true message and mirroring it back to the speaker. This enables the speaker to talk out feelings without being judged or criticized. This form of communication builds a trusting relationship.

For example, if a child comes to you with a problem and says, "My teacher was mean to me today," do not ignore your child. Do not say, "You're always complaining about that teacher." Do not say, "Just do what the teacher says."

Instead, say, "It sounds as if you feel (put in a feeling word)." For example, "You seem angry with your teacher," or, "It sounds like things did not go well today." This tells the child that he or she has the right to feel the emotion, which enables the child to begin to relax and then to think and talk.

Then say, "Tell me more about what happened." This helps the child to reconstruct the problem and discuss details. Listen very carefully.

After your child has described the problem with details and you have asked questions to further define the situation, say, "How do you think you can solve this problem?" or "What could you do differently next time?" This tells your child that you believe that he or she can find solutions to problems. Middle school children are just beginning to realize that there can be several solutions to a specific problem. Some of the solutions are positive, and some are negative. Parents need to teach their children to brainstorm and evaluate the consequences of various actions.

Finally, say, "How can I help you?" Of course you want the child to solve the problem, but you give the message that you are there to help if needed. Teach your child that we can have negative feelings, but we are not entitled to act on them. Instead, we need to seek positive solutions to problems. Children especially need to be taught to use words to solve problems, rather than fighting, and to ask for adult help.

All family members can be taught active listening. The sad fact is that with our busy lives, none of us listens as well as he or she should. Children especially feel that parents do not listen well. To be sure that you are listening well, stop what you are doing. Look directly at your child. Repeat some details to be sure that you have gotten them correctly. It is also nice to end discussions with a hug. This tells your child that even though he or she made a mistake, your love is still there.

For example, Charlie, a sixth grader, speaks with his mom.

Charlie: "Miss Gordon was mean to me today."

Mom: "It sounds like something didn't go well today. Tell me what happened."

Charlie: "Well, I didn't understand how to fill in the map in social studies, so I turned around to ask Billy what to do. Then she yelled at me [children will often use the word "yell" to describe being criticized] to turn around and do my own work. I did want to do my own work, but I had to ask a question."

Mom: "What do you think you could do in the future to prevent this from happening again?"

Charlie: "I don't know."

Mom: "Well, think for a minute."

Charlie: "I suppose that I could raise my hand and ask the teacher for help."

Mom: "That sounds like a good idea. Do you want me to talk to Miss Gordon about your plan?"

Charlie: "No, I think that I can remember."

As simple as this conversation sounds, this is very common thinking for a sixth grader. Seventh and eighth graders know what to do. But they often do not have the self-control that the teachers want. The most important thing to establish with your children is that you are there to listen, to help them think, and to help them solve problems. Do not lecture, repeat yourself endlessly, or talk about your past continuously. These forms of communication turn off children. Your children know what your values for them are. They do not need them repeated in long lectures, only in short sentences.

Another positive form of communication is giving "I" messages (Haim Ginott, 1972). This technique is extremely helpful when you are trying to get your child to cooperate with you. Especially during adolescence, children do not want to cooperate too easily. They normally resist doing what you want them to do and when you want them to do it. If they did not act this way, they would never grow up and be independent. This creates frustration for the parent because when adolescents start to reject their responsibilities or the family rules, parents get angry and yell. Then the children yell. Finally, everyone is angry, and no solution is found.

An "I" message expresses a thought from the point of view of the speaker. It is not a defensive statement, such as "You never do what I ask you to do." This makes a teen even more defensive and hostile because all-or-nothing statements are not correct. When we are angry, we tend to make blanket statements that are inaccurate. Instead say, "I get upset when I see mud on the floor. I need for you to take off your muddy shoes when you come into the house."

Notice: you have expressed your feeling, how the situation affects you, and what you want to happen to prevent the problem from occurring again. There are no defensive statements, no blanket accusations.

"I feel anxious when you and your brothers fight, and the anxiety gets me all stressed out. I need both of you to go to your rooms, close the doors, and do something quiet for twenty minutes so that I can feel better."

"I" messages give the child (or anyone else) the responsibility for changing his or her behavior. It explains how the behavior impacts you, and what you need in order to feel more positive.

Another communication suggestion is to have weekly family meetings. At these meetings, everyone gets an opportunity to speak, one at a time. The purpose is to talk about something positive that happened during the week and then bring up a problem for the family to solve. These meetings are especially helpful when families divorce and there are step-parents and stepchildren. Often, family members have expectations or make assumptions that are not expressed. Then there can be hurt feelings and angry words.

Children routinely compare how their parents treat them with how their siblings are treated. They often perceive unfairness, and when that happens, they take out their anger on their siblings. A family meeting is an opportunity to bring up the issue of unfairness, to examine the reality of it, and to make changes, if necessary.

Mrs. Mathias called to thank me for suggesting family meetings. With four children, there were often a lot of issues. Last week she became aware that her second child, Gillian, was jealous because she felt that her younger sister was given better treatment. Why? Because her younger sister had a food allergy, and Mrs. Mathias had to monitor her food constantly. I explained that when one child in the family has a health issue, the parents have to focus more on that, and the other children may feel slighted. Just talking about this situation helped the children.

If you are angry with your child and tired of repeating yourself, try writing notes rather than engaging in verbal arguments. For example, if your adolescent wants to take out the garbage only when he chooses, leave a written message reminding him to take out the garbage. This may take extra effort on your part, but would you rather have an argument over this all the time? Encourage your child to write notes to you also. Sometimes you can put an "I" message in a note. Or put a love message in a note. Remember the 5-to-1 rule: five positives for every negative comment.

Positive communication is a challenge for all of us in all of our roles in life: as a mate, a child, a parent or a worker (see Figure 10.3). These strategies can help you to keep all of your relationships positive. It takes a lot of thinking and a lot of work, but the rewards are boundless.

Figure 10.3
Developing Communications Skills

1. Express your feelings with "I" messages: "I feel _____ because _____. What I need is _____."

2. Plan a good time to talk. Ask for a good time. Set a date to talk.

3. Don't talk when you are very upset. Cool down. Wait.

4. Plan what you want to say. Practice the conversation in advance.

5. Look for choices, suggestions, options, compromise.

6. Plan a course of action. Follow through.

7. Check back on the success of the plan.

HANDLING CONFLICTS AND ARGUMENTS

1. Discuss *one* issue. Tell your side. Listen to the other person's side.

2. Restate each other's words and position.

3. Listen. Try to empathize.

4. Try to say something positive about the other person.

5. Write letters to initiate a discussion.

6. Watch your tone of voice. Show respect.

7. Work for positive change. Get both sides to agree.

GOOD COMMUNICATION BUILDS POSITIVE RELATIONSHIPS!

Chapter 11

Boundaries, Limits, Expectations, and Consequences

It is easy to understand the concept of boundaries with children when they are young. We teach our children not to go in the street, not to leave the yard, not to open the cabinet under the sink. These boundaries are imposed to protect our children. We are also around them a lot when they are young to enforce these rules. We worry so much about their safety.

Well, parents should worry even more about the safety of their children when they reach middle school. Just because they have grown does not mean that they make decisions based on mature judgment. When children are of middle school age, they need different boundaries set for them. Parents should always know where their children are. It is preferable that they be in a home where there is a parent present to monitor their behavior. Get to know the parents of your children's friends so that you feel comfortable picking up the phone and discussing plans.

When Cindy asked to go to her friend's house for a sleepover on Friday night, her mom called Mrs. Krayer to be sure there would be no boys there and that the parents would be home all night. Cindy's mom also thought it would be clever for her to offer to bring some brownies over so she could actually see who was there. She would also have the opportunity to talk to Mrs. Krayer and form a friendship with her, since their daughters were such good friends.

Young adolescents love to go the mall together. Should they be dropped off to roam around in groups? Absolutely not! This is an age where the group has power over an individual. The threat of shoplifting by children is very real. The danger of selling or buying drugs is also very real. A parent should always accompany a small group of children who want to go to the mall. You don't have to enter every store with them, but your presence will prevent the harmful behaviors. Your children will, of course, protest. Tell them that you are a worrywart, and that you are afraid that they could get into trouble. Tell them that you cannot control your worries, and that this is the only way to pacify them. If you put the onus on yourself rather than saying that you do not trust them or that you do not trust some of their friends, they really cannot be defensive.

Child: "Mom, I would be embarrassed if you come to the mall with Susie, Jane, and me. They'll laugh at me."

Mother: "I'm sorry, honey. I am such a worrywart. I have read that sometimes teenagers get in trouble when they are in a mall in groups, and sometimes they are accused of things that they did not do. I would be so stressed out if I didn't go with you. You are so precious to me."

There is no accusation, no reason for the child to be defensive. And the parent has control over the situation.

Parents also need to impose boundaries when their children watch television, listen to music, or go to the movies. Movies that are "R"-rated usually contain sex, violence, and profanity. A parent may feel that their middle school child has already been exposed to these things. However, the more sex and violence that impressionable youth see, the more acceptable sex and violence become. The more profanity they hear, the more casual they become about using profanity. In decades past, usually girls did not use the "f" word. Today, you can hear girls as well as boys routinely saying that word in the halls of schools.

Regarding television shows and music, parents really need to be aware of what their children are watching and listening to. Sit down and watch your children's favorite TV shows with them. This will give you the opportunity to discuss what you see and to share your values with your children. It is also very important for you to listen to the music that your children listen to. Some groups sound very angry and hostile, and they make liberal use of profanity as well as negative references toward females and authority figures. If you as a parent do not listen to the music, you do not know what your children are exposed to. There are a lot of rock and rap groups today. Some are acceptable to listen to, and some are not. Parents must draw the boundaries to prevent their children from being inundated with negative words and messages.

Mrs. Wallace called again. She needed a lot of parenting advice because she was not a strong-willed person, and her son Howard sometimes got in trouble because he didn't have a lot of self-control. The issue this time was that Howard and his friends wanted to be dropped off at the theater so they could try to get into "R"-rated movies. I told Mrs. Wallace that exposure to sex and violence could bring about more troubling behavior. I suggested that her husband and she tell their son that at age eleven he must have a parent accompany him and his friends to the movies. They didn't have to sit together, but they would watch the same movie. Parents have to be firm and set rules and not allow their children to talk them out of boundaries.

Limits. This is an age of excess: too much food, too many possessions, too much entertainment, too much inactivity. You must set limits for your children. When they were little, you set limits all the time. They could have one cookie or one friend over. Now that they are in middle school, they still need those limits. Setting limits now in a number of areas will help to prepare them for independence and enable them to make wise decisions as they mature.

Bedtimes must be established so that your children can be in optimum form for learning. Some children need quiet time before bedtime in order to be relaxed. Different children need different amounts of sleep. This is an area for negotiation, and once a decision is made, it should be followed every night. Routines add to the stability of our lives.

A major area for setting limits with teens involves the use of the telephone, especially with girls. They can tie up the phone the entire evening, limiting the use for anyone else. What is a good limit? Well, homework should definitely be done before a child can use the telephone. And do not just take their word for it. Check the assignment book, check the homework, check for accuracy. Socializing can be done after work is done. One technique is to use a kitchen timer and limit any conversation to twenty minutes with a fifteen-minute break after that. The worst thing to do is to give a telephone line to a young adolescent, for his or her room, with no monitoring. They do not have enough self-control to be responsible. Remember the power of the peer group? They are drawn to each other constantly. Extra time in the evening would be better spent as family time, playing games, or even watching TV together.

Children also need to respect limits in regard to parents. The parent should have the power to say, "no more arguing," "no more TV," "no more telephone tonight." Unfortunately, many parents today have given up that power to the children. Parents may feel overwhelmed by work and home chores, and they would rather not argue, so they allow children to have their way. Then, when the children go to school, they have difficulty accepting limits there, especially with talking in class. When parents firmly set limits at home, students have more self-control at school.

Mr. Mann had to work so hard to keep Jamie quiet in class. After Jamie would stop talking for a few minutes, he would start up again with another student. Mr. Mann wondered if his parents ever set limits at home. He would have to call them. It is really difficult to teach when a child tries to talk to a friend all the time. If Jamie's behavior didn't change, Mr. Mann would have to discipline him. He would tell Jamie's mother that.

Life is made up of habits and attitudes. When we have a positive attitude about any area of life, we will form good habits. Think about it. When you have a good attitude about your body, you will buy and eat nutritious food and set regular times to exercise. Children thrive on routine and predictability based on habits and attitudes. The family should have dinner together as many nights as possible. There should be established homework times as well as morning and evening routines to help our bodies to function well. Responsibilities within the home should be established. Regularity in a household gives children a feeling of security.

Parents should always have high expectations of their children because children will rise or fall to your expectations. If you expect to see them doing homework and studying at night and, therefore, to get good grades, they will do it. If you let them watch TV and talk on the phone, you are communicating low expectations. If you role model respect at home and tell them that they must be respectful to teachers, whether or not they like them, they will act accordingly. If you speak to them about trying their hardest even if a subject is tough, and tell them that it is the effort, not the grade, that counts, they will develop a work ethic that will carry them successfully through life.

If you remind them to always call you when they are out, they will meet your expectation. If you listen to their problems and not just punish them when they make a mistake, they will feel free to share more with you, knowing that it is more important for you to teach them to solve problems than to punish them.

Joanne got detention again for being tardy to class. She had such a difficult time separating herself from her friends in the halls. But she knew that she could tell her mom because her mom would feel that the school punishment was enough. Her mom would analyze with her how to prevent this problem from happening. Maybe she could get her one of those new popular watches so that Joanne could keep track of the time.

If you expect family members to treat each other with kindness and helpfulness and you do the same, your children will model your behavior. High expectations will bring the best behavior from children. Even though young adolescents will start to stray from your expectations, your resolve to continue to expect the best from them will bring out the best in them.

Consequences. Life is full of consequences, both good and bad. If we do not pay our income tax on time, we have to pay a penalty. We start to teach our children about consequences when they are young, both rewards and punishments. When they become adolescents, they still need those consequences when they break a rule or do something negative. But consequences in adolescence should be appropriate to the misdeed. They should be immediate, and they should be short. Long-term consequences result in anger and resentment, and they usually don't change behavior, which is what you are trying to do with your children.

Thirteen-year-old Charla came in an hour beyond her curfew on Friday, and she didn't call. Her mother was so angry, yelling and calling her names. Charla was grounded—she couldn't be with her friends—for six months. She began to think about how she could sneak out of the house. She was beginning to hate her mother.

How can consequences be appropriate and short term? For Charla, grounding for two weeks is enough. In addition, since she broke a rule concerning safety in the family (if she is out late and doesn't call, she is at risk for harming herself), she should be asked to analyze every room and appliance in the house and write up safety rules for them. If a child throws his or her clothes on the floor instead of putting them in the hamper, the punishment is that the clothes will not be washed by mom anymore. A twelve-year-old can learn to use the washing machine. If a child fails a test, more study time will be demanded and timed before the next test. If a sibling hits another sibling, the child should apologize and also state what led to the hitting and what could be done differently the next time. Then the child should do something helpful for the sibling.

It takes time, energy, and effort for a parent to give punishment to fit the crime. But when this is done, a child learns to think before he or she acts, and a child will be more honest because punishments are not harsh. When this is all done in the spirit of love and devotion from the parents, children will grow up being able to fulfill high expectations.

Chapter 12

Development and the Passage of Time

With any situation that we are presented in life, it is always important to keep in mind the "big picture" and the "little picture." For example, when we start our first job as an adult, we often start at a low level. We may not really like the job, but we know that we have to start there and that, hopefully, we will ascend to a higher-level job that we will like more and that will pay more. So, we tolerate something for a short time because we know that the situation will change in the future.

When we are raising children, we need to keep this same concept in mind. When our child is born, we know that we will have a very difficult three- to six-month period, but eventually the baby will sleep through the night. Before we know it, we will have a toddler running about. And this presents different challenges in that we must watch a toddler constantly, but we know that he or she will be in school all day in a few years.

All human beings go through different stages in life, and each stage presents different tasks to be mastered. Erik Erikson, a personality theorist, divided life into eight stages, each of which presents a major challenge of development. The first stage is from birth to age one, where the development of trust on the part of the baby enables him or her to develop hope, as basic needs are met. At ages two to three, the child struggles with autonomy versus shame and doubt in the toilet training period. If the child succeeds in this task, he or she develops a sense of control over his or her life. At ages four to five when children explore the world, if they are allowed guided freedom they will develop a sense of purpose.

Now we are at the school age of a child. The period from ages six to twelve is a time when a child is judged by his or her school performance. It is very important for children to feel successful and competent in their school tasks, because then they will develop a desire to be industrious and hardworking. But if they meet failure in school tasks, they will feel a sense of inferiority, possibly for the rest of their lives. This is why it is so important for parents to be involved with the school in their children's success.

Mrs. Gorman knew that her daughter Zoey was extremely upset when she again brought home a report card in fourth grade with four Cs. Zoey seemed to be trying, but she just was not learning well. Mrs. Gorman wondered if Zoey might have a learning problem. Another poor report card would discourage Zoey so much. So Mrs. Gorman decided to call the school to ask for a meeting to investigate the source of Zoey's problems.

Notice that this stage goes to age twelve, which is half the time spent in middle school. The next developmental stage occurs right in the middle of these years, further complicating the picture. At ages thirteen to nineteen, adolescents are developing their own identity. Before this time, children know who they are because of what parents and teachers say they are. At age thirteen, adolescents begin to separate from their parents emotionally while they are bonding with their peers. One of the monumental changes that occurs is that peers are telling each other who they are, and adolescents are experimenting with different behaviors to see for themselves who they are. This experimentation can get a child in trouble if he or she does not consider the consequences.

Tom's friends had been pushing him all morning to ask to go to the bathroom and pull the fire alarm. He had thought about it. It was a dare, and he did not want to appear to be scared, and he liked to brag about his accomplishments, especially in sports. He had never been in trouble before in school, but he was very tempted to let his friends know that he was willing to risk it now. He kept thinking about this all morning.

Often, adolescents will experiment with being friends with people that their parents would never approve of. They want to see what it is like to be with people who are different from them. This, too, helps them to seek their own identity. They may be friends with a troublemaker or a jock or a nerd for a year and then let the friendship go. Girls get into arguments with each other and change friendships while they are defining who they are and with whom they want to be. All of these changes are not easy on the adolescent. The turmoil contributes to emotional outbursts and feelings of confusion.

Jessica was in my office crying again. She and Joan, best of friends, had a verbal fight because Sally told Joan that Jessica said that she liked Dylan. Jessica felt betrayed and she was very angry. After a while, I had to draw a diagram to keep straight all the stories about who told what to whom! It is almost comical with girls when they start talking about each other. They go back and forth, loving and hating each other. Jessica and Joan agreed to talk, and I reminded them that good friends keep important information a secret. We talked about being trustworthy and keeping your mouth closed.

It is important for parents to understand that all people go through these stages of development. Each stage that our children go through presents positive and negative behaviors. When our children are in middle school, they are able to think abstractly and be more responsible, which helps us as parents because they can analyze and solve problems. However, they are exploring their identity, and they can be emotionally volatile, which forces us to be patient and tolerant just when we thought that life with them would be easier. In fact, life with children is probably never simple and easy, but that is not why we have children. Human beings need companionship and family. We are gregarious beings. Our children can be a source of love and comfort while they are also challenging every day.

When they reach the age of eighteen, most children are ready to begin their adult lives either by going to college or by moving out and working. They begin to form their own lives, just as we did at that age, and we, as parents, become less involved and less influential. We have many years after they leave to live our lives as we want. If we keep the big picture in mind, that our children will be grown adults on their own some day, we can be more tolerant of the little picture, that our children need a lot of love and time and attention and patience while they are still growing up. It is always helpful for us to keep the stages in our lives in proper perspective so that we can value each stage for the positives that it presents.

Chapter 13

Special Needs Children

Children who have special needs or problems are helped tremendously when parents communicate often with the school and advocate for their children. Students with special needs should learn to become advocates for themselves, which is not easy when facing the formidable power of teachers.

Children who have a problem paying attention in school may have ADD, attention deficit disorder without hyperactivity, or ADHD, attention deficit disorder with hyperactivity. These are neurologically based disorders that a person is born with, and they can be recognized and diagnosed before a child starts school or soon after that. Certain areas of the brain do not have the normal connections they should have. ADD can be an inherited disorder and it causes a variety of problems. If your child has ADD, you need to become educated about the condition.

The areas of the brain that are affected by ADD are associated with various functions. One area helps us to pay attention to tasks, concentrate for an extended period of time, make good decisions, plan ahead, and behave appropriately to a situation. Another area centers around impulsive behaviors, allowing us to wait our turn to speak, to manage our emotions, and to control our anger. The brain also controls whether or not we have normal levels of energy, normal sleep routines, and normal levels of coping with stress (Larry Silver, 1999).

Many people think that paying attention is a passive process. It is really an active process because concentrating involves interacting with a person or object. Because attention is an active process that involves "doing," anything that interferes with that doing, such as misconnections of the brain, interferes with the ability to pay attention. It is natural to avoid working hard on tasks that are difficult, which makes self-control for the ADD child even more difficult.

Children with ADD need a very high level of interest in order to succeed in finishing an assignment, a project, or a chore. This explains why these children can spend long periods of time playing with video games, but they cannot finish a math assignment. Video games are fast moving and exciting, and they give immediate feedback. Homework or household chores cannot compare to this.

One of the most serious problems that ADHD children have is that they do not pick up social cues, and, therefore, they have tremendous problems with friendships. Furthermore, they tend to interrupt conversations and say and do things that are inappropriate. They begin to be rejected socially in elementary school. By the time they reach middle school, they know that other kids exclude them and make fun of them. This can cause a low level of depression, which often displays itself as anger at home (Larry Silver, 1999).

Mrs. Mueller called me because she was worried about her son Todd. He had been in sixth grade for four months and he had not made any new friends. His old friends were starting to reject him. Mrs. Mueller thought that his ADHD was causing the social problems. Todd had been diagnosed in third grade, and life often seemed to be more difficult for him. Mrs. Mueller was hoping that I could start a social skills group for ADHD kids. I told Mrs. Mueller that I would soon be going into classes to distribute a sheet where the students could sign up to participate in several counseling groups that I would be starting. I would keep Todd in mind when I started my groups.

Children with ADD tend to pay equal attention to everything around them. For example, while the teacher is talking, a child may look out the window and see a bird on the grass, hear a girl sneezing, and feel hot in the room. All of these things are given equal attention, and as a result, the teacher's instruction does not receive adequate attention. ADD without hyperactivity is more difficult to diagnose because a child tends to daydream a lot. It is difficult for a teacher to know if a child is listening or not. More girls tend to have ADD, and more boys tend to have ADHD.

Mrs. Leber, an English teacher, came to me. Jane, a new sixth grader, was very quiet and did not participate much. Mrs. Leber could try to bring her out, but what concerned her more was that she wasn't sure if Jane was paying attention most of the time. She was wondering if the school records suggested an attention problem. I told her that I would check it out and get back to her.

ADD children often have very poor problem-solving skills. They tend not to learn from their experiences and, therefore, make the same mistakes over and over. Parents and school staff need to work constantly to teach them to consider the consequences of their actions and to brainstorm solutions.

How is ADD diagnosed? A medical doctor must make the diagnosis. However, a doctor looking at a child for only ten minutes also needs the help of school personnel in assessing possible ADD. There are forms that teachers can fill out that the parent can bring to the doctor. If there is a diagnosis of ADD, the doctor may suggest that the child take medication. There are several different medicines available. When a child truly has ADD or ADHD, the medication really works. The child will need to take the medication until adulthood, when some people become able to control their symptoms on their own. Parents of ADD children also need to provide tight structure and monitoring at home. The combination of the medication with home and school structure enables an ADD child to be successful (John Taylor, 1997).

Many children with ADD also have a learning disability, or LD (John Taylor, 1997). Evidence of learning disabilities appears in several areas of functioning. There are three channels that we learn through: seeing, hearing, and doing. Learning disabilities involve one or more of these areas, and they also involve problems that the brain has processing what is required on a task. Hearing is called the auditory channel. Some children are slow in processing what they hear, and they, therefore, miss teacher instruction. Auditory processing problems make it difficult for a child to get words out of his or her head, thus creating problems in the area of writing. Seeing is the visual channel. Some children have difficulty copying from the blackboard because this involves a multi-step process. For example, consider copying the word "bat." The child tries to hold the word in his or her mind. As she writes, the "b" starts to look like a "d," the "a" looks like a "v," and the "t" looks like an "l." The child sees that his or her work does not look like the word on the board, and he or she feels discouraged. During each step of this process, because it is not a smooth process, there is a breakdown of attention because the work requires sustained, conscious effort.

A child with a "doing" problem, or motor difficulty, cannot carry out a series of physical activities and has difficulty starting conversations and understanding another's physical space. Taking in information and translating it to physical action is difficult.

Difficulty with planning and acting in the proper sequence are the most common contributors to problems of following through. This explains why children suffering from attention problems often forget to check their book bag at the end of the day—it is an action that demands a proper sequence. Problems in following the correct sequence means that this type of child can remember only one command at a time. "Get out your pencils, turn to page twenty-four, and write down every other answer" involves three commands. At home, these children need to be given one command at a time by their parents.

Mrs. Franco couldn't understand why Perry never finished the chores that she asked him to do. He would do the first one, and then he would get involved in playing with something and forget the other two chores. After the doctor explained to her that he had an auditory processing problem, she was more patient, and she asked him to do one chore at a time. It was very helpful for her to know that he was not deliberately ignoring her requests.

How are learning disabilities diagnosed? A team of professionals at school will meet to decide if a child needs testing. There are three kinds of tests: a psychological assessment, an educational assessment, and a speech-language assessment. After the testing is done, the team meets with the parents again, they all look at the scores that the testing reveals, and finally they determine if there is a learning disability. If there is one, various accommodations and an individualized educational plan are made. Parents and the special education teacher will review this every year.

You can imagine that any child who has to struggle with these attention or learning problems may develop emotional problems. After all, school is difficult, parents must help them a lot, and they may be rejected socially. If a child seems to be struggling and has emotional outbursts, outside therapy can be very helpful. Beginning in middle school, group therapy is especially helpful because children can see that they are not alone with their problems, and they help each other, with the guidance of the therapist, to take positive control of their problems.

In addition, parents need to take a continuously active role in helping their children work through their strong areas in order to compensate for the weak areas. For example, if listening is strong but writing is weak, the child can dictate an essay into a tape recorder and then type it on a computer. Word processing skills are important for all of these children. Parents should discuss values and goals with children and allow the children to set their own goals at a pace that they can follow. Because these students need a lot of academic help from their parents, the parents should also be certain to spend fun time with their child, so that the relationship is not a constant drudge from both points of view. Remember that time devoted to helping your children will pay enormous dividends when they are grown and functioning successfully.

Children with attention or learning problems need continuing help in organizing their materials and homework. Notebooks and backpacks should be organized every night, and a system for writing down homework should be maintained daily. Many schools have homework hot-lines where you dial a phone number nightly, and the teacher explains the homework. Parents should listen to this hotline to test the accuracy of what a child wrote down as homework. Work for school should be done at a quiet time and at a table and chair, and it should be done at the same time every day. Consistency helps a child to feel more confident about doing the work. Parents should help children break down large tasks into small steps. Of course, meeting with the child's teachers is always helpful.

Children with special needs require more help from all the adults in the children's lives. The patience and understanding that the adults provide can help the children to be successful in school, and that will raise their self-esteem. A child with an attention or a learning problem can be just as successful in life as anyone else.

Chapter 14

Sibling Conflict

Sibling rivalry occurs in every house where there is more than one child. It is very natural and, when controlled by parents, there is a benefit to it. Through sibling conflict we learn to compromise and we discover that the world will not tailor itself to our needs. When there is more than one child in the family, the children learn that they cannot always have their own way and that they need to share and consider each other.

However, sibling rivalry that is allowed to go unchecked by parents can result in lifelong, devastating effects. There has not been a lot written about the negative impact of sibling conflict, but anyone who thinks back to his or her childhood can still feel the sting of some of those negative interactions. Some adults have absolutely no relationship with their siblings because of cruelty that was inflicted upon them. And some adults develop dysfunctional behaviors from the harsh treatment from their sibs. For example, some people are overly sensitive to criticism their entire adult lives because a sibling was allowed to criticize them on a daily basis.

It was always interesting for me to have a counseling intern, even though it required a lot of time on my part to explain everything. When I met Janet, I could tell she was a real achiever and wanted to be a good counselor. When I began to allow her to talk to students one-on-one in my presence, I noticed that she sometimes would not give the children enough time to think and reply. When I told her she needed to work on this, I could tell she had trouble taking constructive criticism. I guessed that there was a link to her past somewhere. Over time, as we both shared experiences from our personal lives, she told me she was the youngest of four children, and she felt that her older siblings were always correcting her. She knew that she was still reacting as a child when she was corrected, and she knew she had to work on changing her attitude. I admired her honesty and personal insight.

When children reach middle school, negative sibling interactions take on more sophisticated and harmful characteristics. Back in elementary school, children fought over toys or which movie or TV show to watch. In middle school, comments about one's clothes, appearance, friends, skills, and abilities can be very harsh. A brother who starts talking about his sister's weight, if done on a constant basis, will make the girl very insecure about her weight and, therefore, vulnerable to developing eating problems. If a sister teases her brother constantly about his acne, which he already is embarrassed about, his obsession with his acne will increase and his self-esteem will drop. In other words, adolescents can be very hard on each other verbally. If there is still physical fighting among sibs, parents have to stop this. Any form of inappropriate touching can lead to serious problems. If a girl's brother hits her often, she becomes vulnerable to finding a boyfriend who will do the same, and she will allow it because she is used to it. Violence is a learned form of behavior.

Thirteen-year-old Jennifer was getting very upset at the constant harassment that she had to take from her older brother. Her parents weren't home much, and Jake kept telling her that she was fat and ugly, and sometimes he would bump into her on purpose when he would walk by. When she complained to her parents, they would tell Jake to stop, but he never listened. She was getting more depressed and she found that it was difficult to concentrate on her studies. I would have to call her mother and explain to her that Jake's behavior was serious and could have long-lasting effects on Jennifer. This would be a difficult conversation, I knew, because when a teenage boy has this much negative power in a house, it did not develop overnight, and the parents would be in denial. But it was my job to advocate for Jennifer.

Aggression becomes a problem when it is destructive in intent or when children fail to respond to limits set by parents. Frequency, intensity, and motive are important to analyze (Laurie Kramer and Lisa Perozynski, quoted in Harriet Barovick, 1999). You do your children a favor when you teach them to control their impulses and to solve conflicts with words and negotiation instead of violence. We are all born with a certain amount of competitiveness and aggression. However, it is the job of the parent to stop the fighting in a calm and equitable manner. Each child should be listened to and each child's needs are important. Most of all, parents must demand respect in the house. Children must know that they cannot just do what they feel like.

The three parenting styles have a major impact on sibling relationships (Barbara Coloroso, 1995). First, with the laissez-faire parenting style, the children are left to manage their relationships alone. This can produce feelings of hopelessness and frustration in children because the one with the most power, usually the oldest, always wins. Second, autocratic parents try to exert constant control over their children. This can produce silliness and aggression in children when they are left alone. It may also cause rebelliousness when children become teens. Lastly, the best style of parenting is democratic with parental control, where children can discuss their ideas and participate in decision-making, but the parent has the final decision.

If there is a repetitive sibling dispute, parents can create a contract. All parties participate in stating the goals of the contract, the rules, the consequences of breaking the rules, and other details. The contract should be written, signed, and posted.

Mrs. Powell called for some advice. Her children constantly fought over household chores. No one ever seemed content. She needed the help of her children because she was a single mother and she couldn't do all of the work herself. I suggested she sit down with a list of every chore that she needed done. Then, each child would take turns selecting a chore and would sign the contract. Each month they could repeat this meeting so that the children could try a different chore if they felt like it. Mrs. Powell called me a week later to say that it worked! When you involve children in family decisions they tend to be more cooperative.

Here are some group discipline techniques to use: Take away a privilege from all children if family rules are broken. For example, if there is fighting over the television despite an established rule (such as whose turn it is to choose), turn off the TV. Role-play a sibling scene, having each sibling take the other's point of view. This teaches them to look at the conflict from each side and learn empathy. When a parent disciplines, he or she should not be angry, but should talk in a calm manner. Think of acting the way you would at work if there was a conflict.

Siblings can grow up to be best friends or worst enemies. The parents can take credit or responsibility for the future relationships of their children by enforcing positive relationships as much as possible while children are growing up or, negatively, by ignoring sibling conflict. If parents give the energy and attention needed, the entire family can remain close forever.

Chapter 15

Violence in Schools

There are two kinds of violence in schools. The first has occurred since the beginning of mankind: boys or girls have misunderstandings that lead to conflict and possibly a fistfight. In middle school, the professionals spend a lot of time teaching conflict negotiation. We have a conference with the angry students, and each student defines the problem while the other student listens and repeats what was said. Many schools teach peer mediation. Here, the students are trained to mediate with an adult in the room. Usually, when the problem is discussed, a solution is found, even if the solution is that the students agree not to talk to each other. Sometimes, a short fight breaks out in the hall. The adults stop the fight, and the students are suspended for fighting. Adolescents often misperceive what others are thinking or saying about them, and this can lead to a desire to fight when there are misunderstandings or when false rumors are spread among the students.

The second kind of violence is far more serious. Students have brought weapons to school with the intent to kill others, as reported in the news over the past few years. Fortunately, this rarely happens in schools. As infrequent as these incidents are, however, the vivid scenes on television have made us all feel vulnerable and have led schools to develop crisis intervention plans. This new phenomenon in public schools is being analyzed by learning institutions and school systems, and while there are many characteristics that describe a typical shooter, there are exceptions.

The adolescents most likely to bring guns to school to kill others are male, middle-class Caucasians with an average to above-average IQ and no history of serious school problems. They have a very negative self-image and low self-esteem. They do not join any of the usual clubs or activities in school. Others often think of them as nerds or weird, and they themselves feel like "victims" because they are often made fun of in school. Years of harassment coupled with an immaturity and a distrust of people lead them to seek vengeance and what they feel will be an achievement of power and status. They often are not substance abusers, and their act of violence is usually their first and final incident in school. Moreover, they project blame, do not accept responsibility, and they tend to have "all or nothing" thinking. They usually target females and achieving students, as well as athletes and anyone else that they perceive as popular. The important message for parents to give their children is that these avengers always tell others of their plans of destruction. They may write about it, make a videotape, and brag about their violence while they are planning it. Students who hear of such plans should tell adults. The better the adults know the children in a school, the more they can help the troubled students. Obviously, the smaller the school the easier it is to identify those students who need help.

Mr. Ashland, my principal, asked me to come to his office immediately. This was not a normal request. He said that Mrs. Gilford, a teacher, reported that James, her student, had said that he could understand why a student had brought a gun to school (this had been a serious incident that had been reported in the paper). He wanted me to talk to James, of course. I knew that James was different. He was very intelligent, but he dressed strangely, and kids sometimes made fun of him. We had a long talk, and I told James how terrific it was to be unique, as he was. However, it is not easy to be different when you are growing up. James said that he was sorry that he had made that comment, that he could handle his problems pretty well. He had supportive parents, so I was not too worried about him. I invited him to come and see me any time that students teased him and we would celebrate his individuality. He liked that idea. I also called his mother to tell her about what had happened. I suggested that she check out his room to be sure that there were no danger signs, such as magazines or information from the Internet on how to make weapons.

The weapons that these children use usually come from the home. The homes often appear to be normal from the outside, but there are usually dysfunctional behaviors that occur inside. For example, uncontrolled sibling conflict (described in the previous chapter) can be one factor that leads to tremendous anger in a child. Often, the parents of these children who perpetrate violence do not know what their children are doing. There are homes where everyone goes to his or her room, and there is little communication or understanding of what others are doing. These types of parents are often inconsistent in their parenting because there is so little involvement with their children. Thus, the children become further angered at the lack of parental concern. There could be a major cause of stress at home or school that occurs shortly before a school shooting.

The teachers expressed concern to me about John. He seemed strange, he was not very social, and he often did not react when a teacher spoke to him. He was a new sixth grader. I called him to my office. I asked him how elementary school had been for him and how he spent his free time. Then I asked about his family. Although he lived with two parents, he felt that neither of them took much interest in him. His father liked to garden and would spend his free time there. His mother seemed to be busy taking care of the family, and she often had headaches. I asked John if he would like to garden with his dad, and he said that he would. We did a rehearsal conversation where John practiced asking his dad if he could do that. It appeared that his dad was an introvert and hadn't really encouraged John to work with him outside. I also invited John to join in a group that I would be starting to make new friends. I made a note to call his mom and tell her of our plans. John definitely needed some social skills.

The best way for our society to prevent school shootings involves commitment by parents and by schools. Parents must continue to be closely involved in their children's lives until the child leaves home for college or work. Parents need to be honest about their children and seek help when their children are young if they see signs of maladjustment. Meanwhile, schools need to have zero tolerance for violence, providing consequences routinely. Teachers must listen to how students talk to each other and stop any kind of harassment.

Mr. Freen, a new teacher, often stopped in my office to ask questions about classroom management, which I encouraged him to do. This time he was concerned about the fact that he often heard his students insulting each other, using words like "stupid," "ugly," and "gay," or laughing at each other. I explained to him that these days kids hear so many insults on television that they believe it is normal to put each other down. I suggested that he speak to each class and tell the students that he does not want to hear such negative conversation and to tell them why: they need to learn to think before they speak and to be nice whenever possible, because "whatever goes 'round, comes 'round." He would have to explain that phrase. I was glad that he was alert to what children say to each other and sensitive to the fact that they needed to be taught to change these negative social interactions.

Our society has lost much of the reserve and politeness that existed decades ago. Our children hear sarcasm on television, and they often imitate what they hear. We must train our children to be kind and helpful and to have empathy for others. Most people who kill others indiscriminately do not have empathy. Parents and school personnel must work on instilling these character traits at an early age, and they must reinforce them on a continual basis. Everyone chooses his or her behaviors, so we must constantly influence our children to behave in a positive manner toward others. As adults, we must try to role-model helpfulness, consideration, and the use of words that do not hurt others. We must all try to control the natural aggression that is within us.

Chapter 16

Entertain Me Now!

Imagine this: It is a school night, and you want to do anything but attack your homework. You check the TV listings in the newspaper. It doesn't take long. There are only three channels. What other choices do you have? You could read a book or listen to a 45-rpm record on your single-speaker hi-fi. There are no video games, no DVD (digital video disc) players with 3-D programs. There is no Internet.

When I was middle school age, there were only three channels. None of these other entertainment options existed. Today, with astonishing advances in technology, it hardly seems fair to expect your young adolescents to take time off from their twenty-first-century fun and games to do a little schoolwork at home, because they have undoubtedly become members in good standing of the Entertain Me Now Generation. The assault on your child's senses is unrelenting. Video games, with their virtual reality formats, almost literally put your child in the hunt. And it is a hunt—a violent one, too—in many of these games.

Violence also plays a major role in the lyrics of today's rock and rap music, as well as television and movies. So it is not just that the varied forms of entertainment are diverting children from doing their homework today—there is something even more ominous here. Sex, violence, racism, drugs: it is easy to find songs and games and movies featuring any or all of them, and your children don't have to be eighteen or twenty-one.

Take popular music. Do you really know what your children are listening to? Have you ever paid attention to the lyrics? You should, because we've graduated from the Beatles and "I Wanna Hold Your Hand" to rappers saying, "I wanna kill you, bitch." And while sexual lyrics have clearly become more explicit, making love has colored pop lyrics for a long time. Case in point: Led Zeppelin, considered by many fans and critics to be the best "heavy metal" group, had this to say in "Whole Lotta Love": "I'm gonna give you every inch of my love. . . ." The year was 1969.

A popular white rapper recently had a song called "Kill You." In it, he demeans a woman, calls her a bitch, calls her a slut, and threatens to kill her. In another song he proudly reports that he makes "fight music" for high school kids. He sings about beating up his woman. In another song he sings about a bulge in his pants and women staring at it, about people being "heterophobic," about hating a "fag or a lez." A song titled "Drug Ballad" talks about how the singer progressed from sniffing glue and drinking beer to taking Ecstasy and other designer drugs. He says he's graduated to even better drugs as an adult, and he's still got a lot of throwing up to do.

A white rock group produced a song called "Nigger." The lead singer says that people will grow to hate "rock and roll niggers." The group produced another song called "Antichrist Superstar," and the lyrics of one song raised the question: Who says date rape isn't good? A recent survey found that record companies continue to advertise violent songs on television shows and in magazines popular with young audiences, even after industry representatives promised to curb their efforts to market adult-rated music to children, according to the Federal Trade Commission in April 2001. The entertainment industry regularly markets violent movies, music, and video games to children while labeling the products as appropriate for mature audiences only.

For years many black rappers have been criticized for their violent themes. One of the most infamous rappers talks about opening his jacket one day and saying, all right, MF, here I am, now you're coming with me, followed by an explosion of gunfire. He raps about being trapped in a building with the police outside. He then paints a heroic picture of himself as a criminal. On one CD there is a song in which he says that his teachers had told him he was wasting his potential. Their advice was worthless, he claims. He explains how he killed two cops the night before, and he made $10,000 on the deal. He demeans the teachers for telling him that he had to work hard in school to get a good job.

Newspapers have carried stories about the problems "positive" rappers have had gaining radio air time, and their CDs have not sold nearly as well as the "gangsta rappers" who talk about death, violence, anger, and insults. The positive rappers just can't interest very many young people or station executives in nonviolent lyrics.

All of the music your middle school child listens to is not harmful, of course, but it is important to talk about lyrics. Don't be critical of your child. Simply raise some questions about what some of the artists are saying. Also ask what they think about some of the violence and drugs lyrics and whether they feel influenced by them. Music is a major part of their lives, and as parents you should be more actively involved. Shouting "Turn that music down!" is not the kind of involvement I'm talking about. Spend some time listening to the music with them in the car, for example. This setting will be more relaxed than having a formal listening session in their bedroom or the living room. Many artists today, indeed, do write and perform songs that carry positive messages of love.

One heavy metal group, for example, often writes thoughtful, even philosophical lyrics. A hard-driving song talks about a person's battle with paranoia and how he or she is reaching out for help. Another song vividly describes gang warfare and the never-ending loss of young lives. Unlike some of today's songwriters, this group does not glorify violence and sex. A cut from a popular CD talks about self-esteem problems for a young man involved with a woman. Yet another tells about how regular marijuana use affected a man's brain. He took more and more drugs, and now, as the song goes, his friend asks him what has he done to himself. The next time I'll see you, the friend says, you'll be in a coffin.

A number of popular groups that produce softer music, sometimes called "bubblegum," often sing about love, not violence and drugs. "I'll never make you cry. I'll never break your heart," they sing. They sing about unrequited love or broken romances. Some do sing about making love, though not with graphic lyrics. Parents should be aware that there is also this kind of music for their children.

Nothing is left to the imagination, however, when it comes to video games or programs on DVD today. Reality here is virtually there for your child. The names of these games and programs reflect the violent content: "Nuclear Dawn: Nightmare Creatures." And the promos on the covers will further enlighten you. "Prepare yourself for Rune, a brutal third person action adventure on PC CD-ROM," and "Kingdom under fire: young Gurian received his Baptism not by Holy Waters, but by his blood and courage." These are just two of the many provocative introductions. One game cover shows a wrestler smashing two metal chairs down on the head of another. When you play the games, you see blood and gore in scene after scene. Beheadings are frequent. The message is clear: the best way to solve your problems is to kill or maim your adversary. This is the message young adolescents are subjected to today.

As with music, know what your child is watching, whether on CD-ROM or on television, or in movies, two areas where most parents are well aware of the prevalence of sex and violence. Watch the games with your child, and even offer to play one with him or her. Moreover, ask what they think about all of the blood. Entertainment is such a big part of their lives that you must become aware of how they feel about what they are seeing, playing, and listening to.

Unfortunately, it's impossible to avoid sex and violence on television and at the movies. Even movies rated PG will often have violent themes. Remember the days when parents in a TV sitcom slept separately in twin beds? Today's cable nostalgia shows still feature many of these programs, but the major networks carry numerous shows where all of the couples—including unmarried young people—share beds and, in fact, where sex plays a key role in many plots. Some cable stations, of course, routinely air soft-core pornography and leave little to the imagination in the vast majority of their shows.

What about the Internet? You undoubtedly have read about pornography on the Internet and how children have easy access to it. And you probably are aware of the chat rooms where pedophiles meet children. The standing joke is that half of the eighteen-year-old boys in these chat rooms are really fifty-five-year-old men. It is too easy to disguise who you are and to set up a meeting in person. The newspapers have documented cases where this has been done. Unfortunately, some children have been raped in these instances.

Talk to your young adolescent about the dangers of chat rooms and monitor his or her use of the Internet. Be sure to let your child know you are monitoring this, however, so that it does not come as a surprise. You can check which sites your child has been visiting, but, as with music, television, and movies, to build trust you should rely more on talking with your child about these difficult issues than using technology to block access to unsavory information. Again, speak of your fears regarding the negative influence and the possible safety issues.

The problems of sex and violence on television and in the movies and access to adult sites on the Internet have caused great concern among many adults, and congressional hearings have been held on these subjects. Hollywood has pledged to tone down the sex and violence on TV and in the movies, but notice what types of films and shows are in the top ten each week. G-rated movies and family comedies are not likely to be there very often. So the incentive for entertainment moguls to tone down their shows and movies is not overwhelming.

Pay attention to what shows your child watches. The chances are his or her favorite shows will star young people who frequently are having problems with their love lives. Sex—whether implicit or explicit—is certain to play an ongoing role in the plot lines. Virtually all of today's teens watch these kinds of shows, so it is futile to try to keep your child away from them. You might try watching the shows with your child sometimes and discussing the situations portrayed, pointing out reality from fantasy.

The sports entertainment genre of professional wrestling has become one of the biggest influences on today's youth. No longer are the likes of Jackie Robinson, Cal Ripken, Michael Jordan, Mia Hamm, or even Tiger Woods the heroes our kids most want to emulate. The famous, colorful wrestler, Hulk Hogan, who in the 1980s and 1990s was the main attraction of wrestling fans, preaching to children everyday to "take their vitamins and say their prayers," has no impact on today's young fans. Wrestling superstars, such as Stone Cold Steve Austin, The Rock, and The Undertaker have replaced him.

Why should parents care about this evolutionary change? The wrestlers of today are no longer good guys or bad guys, but, instead, they are a mixture of both. Wrestlers now are exhibitionists, whose actions and words are motivated by a desire to represent the fringes of societal values. The violence that wrestling portrays and the sexual innuendo it displays, continue to increase. While Vince McMahon (the owner of the World Wrestling Federation) boasts about the affair he is having with Trish, and the Cat is rearing up to do a strip tease in front of millions of fans, Steve Austin is celebrating his victory in the ring by guzzling down beer after beer.

The Godfather plays a pimp with a following of "ho's." How does he fire up the crowd? By shouting, "Pimpin' ain't easy!" So, what is the result of this mayhem? Kids come to school emboldened by the violence and sex they see in the wrestling matches, and they imitate what they see. Wrestling used to be shown only on Saturday mornings—now, children can watch matches five nights a week. Consequently, parents need to be aware that wrestling, although just another kind of soap opera, can have a harmful effect on their kids' behavior and their attitudes toward sex and violence.

Among boys, watching wrestling has been associated with having started a fight with a date, as well as carrying a gun or other weapon, using chewing tobacco, and taking drugs. Surprisingly, among girls who watch wrestling, many identify themselves as being the initiator or victim of a date fight. The more that girls watch wrestling, the more likely they are to start a fight.

If you see changes in your child's moods, or if he or she seems angry or withdrawn, you should talk with him or her and consider seeking professional help. Too often we have seen a mother and a father on television, shortly after their son has killed another boy, shaking their heads. "We didn't know he was having a problem," they say sadly.

Chapter 17

More about Sex

The expression that "sex sells" seems to be a guiding force in television today. And because our children fill so much of their unstructured time by turning on the TV set, they are being bombarded with sexual images and messages. According to research from the Henry J. Kaiser Family Foundation, more than two-thirds of TV programs in the 1999–2000 season featured sexual content, up from 56 percent two years earlier. Of the characters in television shows having intercourse, 9 percent appeared to be under the age of eighteen, and 23 percent were between the ages of eighteen and twenty-four. The largest increase occurred in situation comedies, where 84 percent of episodes had sexual content. A popular late-night show (how many children have television sets in their bedrooms?) revolves entirely around sexual relationships. There are ninety-seven characters in the latest season, and each character is on for a short time, just enough time to begin flirtation and a sexual relationship. Each episode has three story lines involving a high school relationship, a college relationship, and one post-college. The story can go from literally "hello" to "don't you want to take off my clothes?"

The constant message of this ubiquitous entertainment is that sexual relationships are normal behaviors for young adolescents. This becomes a self-fulfilling prophecy. After all, the more that children—or anyone else, for that matter—hear a message, the more comfortable they become with it. The natural sexual interest that hormones stimulate in boys and girls has now become an urge that they can act upon. We see this in several ways.

Those popular school dances in middle school have now incorporated a new style of dancing called "freak dancing." Couples can be front-to-front, legs intertwined, bending, or standing up. Or, the more popular form is a couple front-to-back, as close as possible, moving and writhing while their bodies are touching each other. It looks like sex with clothes on, and it can be anonymous because the couple is just dancing. They are not particularly interested in each other. Of course, this drives the chaperones crazy.

At the May dance—doesn't the spring seem to bring out wild behavior—things were going smoothly. Suddenly, a large crowd surged around several couples who were freak dancing. The administrator and teachers tried to break through the crowd, but it took a while because everyone was screaming or yelling, and the music was so loud. When the principal finally found her way to the middle, she immediately stopped the sexual dancing of three couples. The rest of the crowd booed, but they knew that this was not allowed. Chaperones at dances have had to become even more vigilant because of this freak dancing.

Even more alarming is the fact that among adolescents oral sex has now become an accepted, commonplace activity. This is a phenomenon that has occurred in the past few years. Oral sex in recent years has become a more common topic in the newspapers, which has taken this practice out of the bedroom and into common conversations. With impetuous adolescents, what is on the mind may soon become an action that they pursue.

Peer pressure also has an enormous impact on experimentation with oral sex. Because many boys and girls are talking about it so much, others become curious. Then, if Alice tells her friend Betsy that she has done it, it becomes acceptable to Alice. None of the girls wants to admit that it may not be a pleasurable experience for her, so she brags about it, which makes other girls want to try it.

Where is this happening? In unsupervised homes after school. In most neighborhoods, there is a home where there is no adult present until dinnertime. All the kids know which homes are free of parents, and they gather in groups. Boys ask girls to perform oral sex on them, and it doesn't mean that they are dating. Any boy can ask any girl, and this is considered to be an acceptable request. They go off to a bedroom or to the basement. When they return, and they are both smiling (of course, the boys are really beaming), then others feel that it is OK for them to do the same. Whereas boys and girls used to gather together to watch TV or play video games, they now have this added activity that at any time a boy and girl can go off to have oral sex, and then return to the TV or the video game.

I received a call from my principal to come to the office immediately. I could not believe the story. One of my girls had given oral sex to a boy—in the bathroom in school. The adults were all astonished. Another girl had gone into the bathroom and discovered this activity and reported it to the principal. The sad thing was that my girl was not popular or attractive, and she was searching any way she could for a boyfriend. Not surprisingly, this was an eighth grader who was tired of feeling as if she was not part of the crowd. Both students were suspended, of course. But the talk went around the entire school. As you might expect, people made fun of the girl, but the boy's reputation was enhanced among his friends. The double standard still remains. The girl's mother agreed to send her to counseling immediately. Because this was such a serious issue, and I knew that the girl would be in counseling, I didn't get involved in a discussion. But I felt deeply saddened.

What is additionally troubling is that girls do not know they can get a sexually transmitted disease from oral sex, including HIV. Teens today are often replacing sexual intercourse with oral sex, which they regard as another form of petting. Of course, young people generally believe they are almost immortal and are not afraid to take risks. And girls whose self-esteem is really low may not care at all that they can contract a disease or even ruin their reputation by having oral sex with many different boys. Often these are girls whose fathers abandoned them and they are desperately seeking male attention. The more troubled girls seek out many partners to prove their self-worth and popularity. Unless a mother is willing to intervene and begin strong counseling with someone who is experienced in this, these girls can develop an addiction to alcohol or drugs as they try to assuage their poor self-image.

Even more alarming are the drinking parties. Again, often in unsupervised houses, teens are starting in middle school to go to parties where there is alcohol. Often, boys want to get the girls drunk so that they can take advantage of them. And there are many new drugs that can cause a person to become unconscious. Some boys slip these drugs into a girl's drink and then have sexual intercourse with her. Moreover, a girl wouldn't even know if a boy wore a condom or not. And she may become so embarrassed about what she did that she will not seek help. A good rule to tell girls: never put down a soda you are drinking so that a boy will not have a chance to put a drug in it!

Clara came to me, and she looked very disturbed. She started crying uncontrollably, and I had to let her have a few minutes to compose herself. Finally, she told me what happened. She had been at a party a few weeks ago, and she had become so drunk she thought she had passed out. There were no parents at the house. For the past few days, she felt an itching and burning in her vagina, and she was afraid to tell her mother because her mom would yell at her and ground her. So many children today do not understand that when there is harm or danger involved, parents have to be informed in order to protect their children. I immediately invited the nurse to join us. She asked Clara if she thought that some boy had had sex with her. The nurse explained that we had to protect Clara, that a sexually transmitted disease could cause permanent damage, and that her mother had to be called so that she could be examined by a doctor. Of course, Clara only cried more and more. I felt so sorry for her. This would be a horrible experience that she would never forget. I had to impress upon her mother to try to treat her gently, so that Clara would be open with her. And she must take her to counseling as well. I was thankful that I was not an adolescent today.

Even when parents are home during a party, kids can be drinking or taking drugs. One of my female students told me that while parents are inside, kids go in and out, and outside is where alcohol is being consumed. Or, if the parents are on one floor, the illicit activity is taking place on another floor. Kids know how to be sneaky. The constant drumming of the music, often with lyrics that are sexual in nature or that call women bitches and whores, adds to this atmosphere. When a girl dances to a song that denigrates women, and she laughs while she is dancing, what message does this give to boys? The bottom line is a tremendous lack of respect that some boys develop for females.

Many schools have a sex education unit in health class in the eighth grade. Of course, a parent must sign a permission form for any individual child to be able to attend this course. One of the techniques that teachers use in order to properly inform teens about the risks of sexual behavior is to ask students to write questions on index cards, and the teacher will answer the question. They are fascinated about pregnancy and the process involved. They ask a lot of questions about birth control, and they really do not know a whole lot about it. They want to know about the hymen and menstruation. Here are some sample questions that were given to me:

Can you get pregnant if you have intercourse standing up?

Why can't men get pregnant?

Is being a *homosapien* like being a homosexual?

Why are girls mean when they have their period?

If a girl pours cola into her vagina after intercourse, will she prevent pregnancy?

Why don't boys have periods?

Can a woman bleed to death after her period?

Is it considered losing your virginity if you stick a tampon in?

Can you get pregnant from having "dry sex?"

What is the difference between pubic hair and the hair on your head?

If pubic lice is spread during intercourse, how does it get on a person's genitals?

If blood causes a penis to become erect, why doesn't a person bleed to death?

If a woman is pregnant and she sneezes hard, could the baby come out?

Will the baby be bruised if a mother has sex in the ninth month? Wouldn't the head be lopsided?

If a man has anal sex with a woman, could she get pregnant?

Is oral sex considered sex?

Can a female get pregnant if she is lying next to a man that is having wet dreams?

Does a man's penis get bigger as they get older?

Will eating certain kinds of food before sex prevent pregnancy?

As you can see, teens are woefully ignorant about sex, but they are experimenting with many forms of sex. It is imperative for parents to talk to their children about this. Children should be told the dangers of any form of sex, and they need to have accurate information about those dangers. Meanwhile, parents should look for books that give intelligent information. Most importantly, parents need to have discussions, to ask questions, to listen, and to make their children feel comfortable talking to them. Sex is probably the most difficult topic for a parent to discuss. A parent has to overcome his or her embarrassment and be courageous. In today's climate of free sex, not to do so is to endanger our children. It is critical to give this information to both boys and girls.

Chapter 18

You Are a Parent, Not a Friend

In a word, parenting skills today are a mess! Parenting is also much more difficult than anything known in the past. In fact, parenting used to be relatively simple, for two reasons. First, families used to live near relatives and close friends. Families would often have dinner with grandparents and aunts and uncles. They would spend weekend time together. The benefit of this was that if Johnny or Suzie were misbehaving, besides mom and dad lecturing and disciplining, grandma or an aunt would reinforce what the parent had said. Second, before this generation, roles were well defined. A father was the provider in the home. The mother took care of household duties. Imagine not having a washing machine or dryer! Imagine having to go shopping for food several times a week and having to make all food from scratch! Women had to stay home because there were none of the modern conveniences that we have today. Also, of course, the entertainment industry mostly steered clear of behaviors that were extremely aggressive or sexual. And, there were not large peer groups that could wield tremendous influence on a child, only a few neighborhood friends.

What do we have today, in contrast? Families move a lot. People change jobs or are transferred. Gone is the extended family. Roles are all intertwined today. Fathers and mothers both work for many reasons. One reason is that we are such a materialistic society that we all want more money to buy more things. Television shows us a vast array of items to buy. Especially with young adults, there seems to be an urge to have the latest in fancy appliances, cars, and entertainments. A regular television set will not suffice for some people today because DVD (digital video disc) players are so much more interesting. CD (compact disc) players have replaced tape recording machines in cars, and CDs cost more than tapes. To their benefit, women now can enter any professional field, and many women are now doctors, lawyers, and accountants. Thus, the roles of father and mother incorporate all duties: cooking, paying bills, shopping, and disciplining the children. The problem is that many moms and dads are so tired after working, shopping, and cooking that they do not have enough energy to monitor and discipline their children.

It does take a tremendous amount of time and energy to raise children. When they are toddlers, children are very active. This is a time when they need to learn boundaries: what is acceptable and what is not. Have you seen a two-year-old in a store who is running around touching everything while the parent is standing there looking at a magazine or an article of clothing? This is the age where children should learn that when mom or dad says "no," they mean it! A parent who is doing the right thing will say, "If you touch that again, we are going to the car immediately, and we're going home." This is how a child learns self-control—from the parents exerting physical control when the child is young. If, however, the parent does nothing, the child learns that all forms of behavior are acceptable.

When children reach elementary school, their behavior reveals whether they have had parents who have monitored them and been firm about rules, or whether they have been allowed to run wild and, therefore, have little self-discipline. Many parents today just want to have a good time in life. They don't want to use energy to discipline and teach children. Because life was so much more difficult in previous generations, parents willingly accepted sacrifice and hard work. They felt proud although weary to work hard to make their lives better. Today, there are many conveniences, and there is so much entertainment. We are all spoiled by this. But when young children are not given firm foundations in acceptable behavior, they bring problems of lack of control to the school. Teachers now have to teach behavior limits, as well as reading, writing, and arithmetic. If teachers have to spend more time disciplining in the classroom, obviously, instruction time is lost.

Another reason that parents have become so lax about parenting is that they feel guilty because they are working and are away from their children. Especially if parents do not get home until dinnertime, they are already tired from work, and demanding children are difficult to deal with. So, they relent on rules, they feel guilty because they do not have the energy to play with and talk with their children, and they let their children do almost anything. And then, parents go out and buy more toys to make up for the time not spent with children.

So, by the time those children get to middle school, parents have often not taken the time to teach some basic thinking skills. Children need to be taught good decision-making skills. How is this done? By talking to children about their day, their problems, their challenges. By asking them what choices they have to solve a problem. What would be the outcome of each choice? Which choice will you make? When will you do it? Young adolescents especially need to be taught so-called refusal skills. Because the peer group has so much power, children should be taught how to refuse invitations that could bring them trouble or harm. How is this done? By finding out what pressures the child is under. What can you say to avoid going to an unchaperoned house? What can you say to avoid taking a drink of alcohol? Let's practice some lines.

No thanks, I'd rather not.

I tried that once, and it made me sick.

My parents are really on my case, and, if they found out, I'd be grounded for life.

I have to go to the dentist today.

I have a paper due tomorrow, and if I don't get it in, I'll get a "D."

I already made plans with someone.

I don't feel good. I'm going home. I feel like throwing up.

I'm not interested now.

If a parent is not a strong person and does not assume the role of parent, these skills will not be learned. You can't be a friend *and* a parent. The roles are different. A friend may not be vigilant about what is good for you and what is bad for you. Moreover, a friend wants to play. However, a parent wants to raise a child who will be smart about him or herself and will have the skills to be successful in life. A parent wants to raise a child who will have goals and ideals. A parent monitors that which could be harmful and weeds it out. A parent is not afraid that a child will become angry, throw a tantrum, or say that he or she hates a parent (it's only for the moment, of course). A parent has strength and courage and, most important, is a role model for the child.

A smart parent understands the effectiveness of rewards and punishments. Rewards always work better than punishments, just as the old adage says that honey attracts more bees than vinegar. It is important to recognize that rewards and punishments only work if they are immediate and appropriate. Promising a child a reward at the end of the year for good grades will never work. For children, next weekend is a long time away. The end of the year will take forever.

I couldn't believe Mrs. Blank. She was concerned about her son's low grades. She said that she promised him a new bike in June if he raised his grades. It was currently October. I explained to her that if she wanted to see a change in grades, she needed to provide weekly rewards. We discussed the rewards that her son might like and a contract that he could live with. She agreed to come in, and the three of us could have a meeting. I hoped that she had the will to persevere, so that she could help her son to change his negative attitude and habits.

Parents probably focus more on punishments than rewards. And, there are many times when consequences have to be given for bad behavior. I have heard of so many punishments that are absolutely inappropriate because they have nothing to do with the crime. If grades are low, grounding and taking away entertainment don't solve the problem. In fact, this only makes children angry and determined not to be cooperative. If grades are low, then parents should force their children to spend time each night at a table doing homework. If children are fighting, they should be punished equally. They should also be separated on different floors of the house for the remainder of the day. If a child does something wrong, he or she should be taught to apologize. If a child does not do what a parent asks, and the parent asks several times, a child should be asked to write a paper about why it is important for all members of a family to be helpful and cooperative. The punishment should be immediate and short-term. Then, normal relationships should return. Hitting as a form of punishment for young adolescents is totally inappropriate. What hitting teaches is that aggression works. A hitting parent becomes a role model for a child who then hits others at school. And it is always important for parents to say that they love their child even when he or she misbehaves.

When Martha showed me the marks on her arm and told me that her dad had hit her with a belt when she was arguing with her brother, a shiver went through me. I knew that I had to call Child Protective Services. I had to get more details to report. The officials would come out to the school to interview Martha, and then they would go to the home. If her dad thought that I reported him, he might get angry at me and harass me. It was all a bad situation, but I had to follow the law and report this. I explained to Martha that her father was wrong to do what he did and that she should tell me if it happened again. I knew that she felt better telling me, and she felt that I could protect her. I also knew that some of the social workers would work with these parents and teach them more effective disciplinary tools. I hoped that we would be assigned one of these people to talk to Martha's dad. It was difficult to report the beating to CPS, but I had to do it. I thought about how much help this might give to Martha.

Home should be a place where a child feels safe and loved. If you listen to your child and teach good decision-making skills, your child will be less inclined to lie to you. If you are not ready to punish, the truth comes out more easily. Parents also should be available when their children need them. As children move into adolescence, parents need to become more flexible with their time so that they can be with their children easily. Children must be taught to be assertive, asking for what they want in a firm but positive manner. They also should be taught that they have a right to express their opinions, to make and refuse requests, to be treated fairly, to express annoyance, to make mistakes, and to ask for help. It is only through good dialogue with your children that you will learn whether they are assertive.

Parents also need to be creative in restricting television viewing and excessive time spent on other entertainment. There are many fun activities that a family can do together or a child can do alone. Make up a scavenger hunt for a weekend family activity. Bake together. Look at photo albums. Write a letter or a poem. Put on a puppet show. Do jigsaw puzzles. Have a family talent show. Plan a vacation together. Play games. Find a new recipe for dinner. Have everyone clean a room together. Get a joke book and read it aloud. Go to a museum. The more you broaden your children's activities, the more interesting they become and the more interesting their lives are.

Because some parents are so lax in raising their children, we have children today who exercise too little, weigh too much, and sleep too little. We all know how important it is to take good care of our bodies so that we can all function well each day. Many parents don't take good care of their own bodies, let alone the bodies of their children. There are many articles in the newspapers about how overweight the American public is becoming. Fast-food restaurants are everywhere, and easy-fix meals are in abundance in the groceries. People are consuming too much fat, sugar, and carbohydrates. If you are a weak parent, and you drive by a fast-food restaurant and your child starts whining for French fries, of course you will give in. If you are a weak parent, and your child starts whining because he or she wants to stay up late to watch TV, of course you will give in. And if you are not concerned about your own body, and you know that your child and you are getting no exercise, of course you will not start a regimen of taking a walk. Do you give your child soda and cookies for a snack because they demand it? Do you bring all kinds of candy and high-fat foods into the house because your child demands it? Are you afraid to say "no?" Are you afraid of tantrums? Are you afraid of your child crying? If the answers are "yes, yes, yes, yes, yes," then you are a wimp parent.

Eventually, children have no respect for wimp parents. Children learn that they can manipulate them. They can lie to them. They can put the blame for bad behaviors on others. They can put the blame for low grades on the teacher. They can put the blame for drinking alcohol at a party on their friends. They know that they don't have to be responsible. They know that they can bamboozle their parents. They know that they can get what they want. Later, what happens when they grow up? When they don't get what they want at work, they may quit their jobs. When they don't get what they want in their marriage, they may get a divorce. When they don't get what they want out of life, they may take up drinking. They don't become strong people. They become sad, weak people. They may hate their parents in the end because they have become blamers in life. They don't accept responsibility, and they don't set goals for themselves. They think that life should bring them what they want.

Be a strong parent. Teach your children boundaries, rules, and values. Monitor what they do and whom they are with. Check with the school about their progress. Make them go to bed at proper times. Don't bring food into the house that is not good for them, except in small amounts or on special occasions. Make them exercise. Do it together. Ride bikes. Take walks. Talk to your children. Listen to them. Set consequences for inappropriate behavior. Compliment them. Hug them. Love them.

Chapter 19

Can Middle School Students Be Stressed?

We all know how stressed adults can be in our modern world. Jobs are stressful. Traffic is really stressful. Children are stressful. What isn't stressful today? When you look at how simple the life of a middle school child appears to be, though, you probably can't imagine that they have too much pressure at so young an age. Try imagining harder.

What are they stressed about? In school, they have to organize their materials, do class work, adjust to different teachers, follow rules, do homework when they really want to be entertained, and more. Probably the biggest source of stress is relationships. The social skills of young adolescents are so undeveloped that they keep practicing on each other, insulting each other, being friends, being enemies, and being totally stressed about the entire process. Then they come home, and their parents, who are also stressed, make more demands on them when all they want to do is watch television. Then they have to deal with their siblings, who probably cause them discomfort every day, even if they get along.

What can a parent do to help? Many things. First, recognize that your children are living with a lot of stress each day, whether it is academic, social, or familial. Second, realize that different people react to stress in different ways. Some of us have easy natures and can "go with the flow," while others react to every little thing that happens. Look at your children. Which of these categories do they fall into? When your children come to you with a story about the day or about a problem, take the time to listen to them, try to understand what they are living through, help them with thinking logically, and teach them good decision-making skills. Children need a lot of help thinking because they cannot think abstractly until they are about ten years old. We already know that boys can be impulsive and girls can get emotional (certainly the opposite is true also). So where does thinking come in? It has to be guided by parents.

Another thing you can do is to find out what bothers your children, what pushes their buttons. Teach them about that. We all have our sensitivities and vulnerabilities. Help your children to understand themselves so that they can begin to have control over what annoys them and what their reactions are. If you have a child who is very sensitive to teasing, work with that child. Teach him or her that it is important not to react to teasing, that this invites more teasing. This is an essential fact about behavior among children. Those who react to taunts are going to be taunted. Those who ignore taunts will eventually be left alone. Children don't know this unless they are taught it. Then you could even do some role-playing activities where you take turns as the one who teases and the one who is teased. A role-playing exercise always makes us more comfortable with a situation that we dread.

Then, teach your children that when a stressful situation occurs, they have a choice about how they can think about it. They can think that it is horrible, or that it is no big problem. How we interpret a situation determines how we feel about a situation. If we think that something is terrible, we will feel bad about it. If we think that something is innocuous, then we do not have a negative feeling. Our feelings then determine our actions. If we are unhappy or angry, we will do something that reveals our feelings. If a teacher tells Jimmy that she wishes that he would do his homework regularly, and Jimmy interprets this as an insult and he is angry, he may leave the room and slam the door, causing him to get a detention. Our feelings then become a part of our body. If we walk around angry, our body systems are affected in a negative way. For adults, this can lead to some serious illnesses. For children, this can lead to body complaints, aches and pains, not feeling good. Thus, our feelings come from our beliefs, and if we change our beliefs, we can change our feelings. This is an extremely complex concept. It will take a while for you to understand it, and it will take longer for your children to understand it. Every time that you or your children are angry, you can trace the anger back to a belief, perhaps an irrational belief. If you can change the belief, you can change the feeling. This is one of the most helpful concepts that a person can learn.

For example, if your boss asks you to do extra work, and he or she is entitled to do so, you could become angry. The reason for this is that you are telling yourself that your boss is a terrible person for putting extra burdens on you. However, if you change your thinking, and tell yourself that once in a while your boss is going to ask this, then you do not have to get angry on top of having to do extra work. Developing patience and acceptance of situations save us from a lot of aggravation.

If your child comes home complaining that his teacher gave him a big project to do, and the teacher is too demanding, you can help your child work through this thinking. Tell him that teachers are supposed to give major projects in order to teach students how to do long-range planning and how to budget their time. Tell him that in the world of work this also happens, and that school is the place to acquire this skill. This is not a bad thing but, rather, a fact of life. There is no reason to be angry. Start planning. Let's look at the assignment and divide it up. Then we'll put it on the calendar. Do you need to go to the library? Can I help you with any of it? Do you need more information? When life throws a challenge at us, the best way to handle it is to start managing it and not let it manage us. Teach this to your children. Then they won't blame the world for things that are difficult in their lives. Instead, they will solve problems and take positive actions.

Recognize the signs of stress and teach these to your children. These include a lot of physical symptoms. A person may become irritable on a regular basis. There may be sleeping problems or complaints of physical illness, such as stomachaches or headaches. A child may be worried or confused a lot. There may be a general agitation. There could be a desire to escape the normal routine.

Once you teach your child about how to understand stress, the next step is to acquire techniques to relieve stress (see Figure 19.1). There are many possibilities. One way to handle stress is to schedule our lives so that we have a balance of work time, exercise, proper nutrition, time to relax, and adequate sleep. I cannot state strongly enough how important it is to have balanced lives and to take good care of ourselves in order to handle the stresses of life. This is the very first concept of stress management. With adequate sleep, food, and exercise, it is easier to accept each day's challenges.

Teach your children how to calm down when they get angry. There are suggestions such as counting to ten, breathing slowly, moving to another place, or talking to someone. Visualization or meditation can help. Visualization is a process of taking ourselves mentally to a place of beauty, perhaps the beach or the mountains. Imagine what everything looks like, including sounds and smells. Take a few minutes to go outside the moment and go to a place that is relaxing. Meditation is a process of breathing deeply and saying two syllables over and over, trying not to think. Some people meditate on a regular basis, which has been shown to improve their health. Another technique to relieve stress is the gradual flexing and relaxing of body muscles, starting from the head to the toes, or vice versa.

Finally, teach your children to monitor what they are thinking. We all

Figure 19.1
23 Easy Ways to Relieve Stress

1.   Prepare for the morning the night before.
2.   Write it down.
3.   Use time wisely.
4.   Ask for help.
5.   Break large tasks into bite-size portions.
6.   Be aware of decisions that you make and their consequences.
7.   Believe in yourself.
8.   Ask a friend for a hug.
9.   Practice breathing slowly.
10. Listen to music that is soothing.
11. Do the job today.
12. Stand up and stretch.
13. Exercise every day.
14. Remember that stress is an attitude.
15. Remember that you always have options in solving problems.
16. Get enough sleep.
17. Watch a movie and eat popcorn.
18. Always have a plan "B".
19. Smile.
20. Find support from others.
21. Use a calendar to organize your work.
22. Talk about what bothers you.
23. Develop patience!

talk to ourselves every day. Much of what we say can be negative, such as, "I can't do this," or "This is a waste of my time." Negative thoughts add stress to our lives. Teach your children positive coping statements. These include the following:

Stay calm. Relax.

What she says doesn't make any difference.

I can work out this problem.

I can ask for help.

If I mess up, it's OK.

This will soon be over.

It won't help if I get mad.

I don't need to prove myself to him.

People won't act the way that I want them to.

I can control myself.

It's too bad that she is acting this way.

I have a great plan for this weekend.

I'm getting tense. I'll relax my muscles.

Boy, there's something wrong with him.

I'm not going to be pushed around. I'll be assertive.

We all make mistakes.

I'm a winner anyway.

I guess that I need to be more responsible.

Learning about stress is important for everyone. The sooner you teach these ideas to your children, the earlier they will be able to manage their lives in a positive way. They will need these techniques throughout their lives!

Chapter 20

Accepting Your Child

The most important gift that a parent can give a child is total acceptance and love. This has never been easy for parents. Often, we want to live vicariously through our children to compensate for disappointments in our own childhood. We want our children to learn from us and not make mistakes. If a child is not accepting of a parent's wishes or demands, that child can begin to develop the roots of low self-esteem. Some parents go so far as to badger their children to be the kind of persons the parents want them to be, or the parent will totally denigrate and ignore a child. The toll of the pain and suffering is enormous.

Most parents are amazed at how different their children are from each other. This is because genes can reach back several generations. Most of us do not know relatives generations back, so the traits that we see in our children are sometimes foreign to us. Of course, the environment also shapes who we are and who we become.

There are many opinions about how much of ourselves is inherited and how much is shaped by environment, anywhere from 50/50, to genetics or the environment having a 75% effect on who we are. Most people can recognize some personality traits that are apparent at birth. Some children seem to be very restless and irritable from the beginning, while others are calm sleepers. This is the first important factor to understand. We are born with a certain temperament. Parents can find books about basic temperament and how to best raise children with certain tendencies. For example, some children seem to be very sensitive to sensual stimuli. They react to sound and noise more than others do.

These children need to be kept in a calmer environment that will not irritate them, allowing them to develop more peacefully. Other children seem to be very active and alert and enjoy lots of stimulus. These parents will probably have to monitor these children very carefully when they are toddlers because they can get themselves into a lot of trouble. So, there are some basic personality traits that come at birth, and it is important for parents to accept the individual nature of each child.

My neighbor had just given birth to her first child, a boy. When she came home from the hospital, she told me that her baby was the only one crying constantly in the hospital. She had asked her doctor about it, and he said that some children are born with more intense natures, and perhaps her son was one of them. I suggested to my neighbor that she try to be patient, that the baby was crying for a reason, and that she should get extra help in caring for him for a few months. I offered to do whatever I could.

There are many kinds of talents that can be inherited. Musical and artistic talents are good examples. A child can display a penchant for music by age four, for example, picking out a musical tune on a toy piano. Artistic talent may reveal itself in early elementary school. Children with these talents would benefit greatly from early training and instruction. However, children who do not have such artistic or musical talent can certainly learn to play a musical instrument or learn to draw or enjoy art activities. But a parent who pushes a child to be a piano virtuoso when the talent is not there can create tremendous pressure on a child, and that may bring about symptoms of anxiety.

Lynn came crying to me. Her mother was making her practice piano two hours a day, and Lynn hated it. Her piano teacher had said that she would have to practice that much to be as good as some of her other students. Lynn did not want to do that. I couldn't call her mom and tell her to stop doing that. So I worked with Lynn on finding an advocate in her family and being assertive in how she spoke to her mother. She needed an uncle or a grandmother who could understand her and talk to her mother. That was all that I could do in this case.

Athletic ability is a major concern to many parents. Again, some children show signs early of being coordinated and talented in sports. Most communities have soccer programs that children can join by second grade. Kids have lots of fun with this. They love their uniforms, weekly practices, and games. All children can run, and some can kick a ball well. However, a problem can emerge when children are in about sixth grade. This is a time when the more athletically talented kids join select teams. These teams are more competitive and travel farther for their games. This begins the first weeding out process, the first acceptance or refusal, the first highs and lows of competitive sports. Moreover, this change becomes a challenge for parents themselves. There have been occasional articles about parents who are so rabid in their support for their child or their team that the parents themselves can become aggressive and violent. These parents have lost sight of the fact that their child is supposed to be having fun and learning teamwork. These parents may act as if it is *their* life that is being affected, and they set a very bad example with their behavior. Good sportsmanship is not important to these parents. Only winning is.

What happens when a child has no or little athletic ability? Some parents, particularly if one of the parents is athletic, will not accept this. They may push their child into lessons and teams that the child wants no part of. While the parent cannot accept the child's limitations, the child cannot accept the parent's pressure, creating a scene of conflict and misery for some. When a parent gives the message that the child is not OK being the way he or she is, the child's self-esteem plummets. This creates tremendous stress for the youngster, and unrelieved stress can manifest itself in symptoms of anxiety. The child may have stomachaches or have trouble sleeping. Or he or she may begin to do poorly in school and become irritable. This can be a real test of a parent: to accept a child who is not athletic. The child already suffers in school because children who are not athletic are often teased in school. Every PE class is a reminder of incompetence and an opportunity for harassment. A parent of a nonathletic child should help the child to develop other interests. Frequently, these boys become skillful in the use of computers, and the girls may also like computers or develop other hobbies. It is really important for parents to be sensitive to this, because each child needs to feel competence in at least one area of his or her life.

Poor Charlie! He had a horrible time in PE because he could not compete. The other boys often made fun of him. Sometimes they would call him "gay" because he was not athletic. I informed the PE teacher about how sensitive this was, and I worked with Charlie's mom to help him to find competence in some other area and to support him. I knew that time would help, and that as students become older, there are other activities that bring them together. Usually, this teasing lessens in the middle of high school. But in middle school, children who are not athletic may suffer. They should be able to agree with their tormentors and try to laugh about it.

Another area of concern is academic ability. Again, this is often inherited. Even though all children can learn a lot in school, basic IQ is inherited. So are learning disabilities and attention deficit disorder, or ADD. These traits tend to run in families. Many adults today are realizing that they have ADD and are seeking medication to help them focus and organize better. In our world, we need all kinds of people to do all kinds of jobs. If a child is not highly academic, and getting good grades is difficult, a parent then should provide any kind of help that is needed, and then finally accept the child for the grades that he or she gets. Many of us are good in math but not in English, or vice versa. When we are in school, we all need help in our weak areas, and we need to feel that this is OK.

Too many children tell themselves that they are stupid and they can't learn. They *can* learn a great deal in school, but some of them need help in understanding how to learn and in accepting their difficulties along with their successes. Pressuring an average student to go to an Ivy League school is an exercise in futility and cruelty. Each child should be programmed for success, which means that his or her strengths and weaknesses are analyzed, accepted, and planned for. Of course, all parents should have high academic expectations. But some parents are critical of any grade that is below an A. When a parent has this kind of attitude, a child learns to become secretive and begins to keep information from parents. This can be the beginning of the breakdown of the child/parent relationship.

Mrs. Jasper called me when report cards came out. I knew that she would. She would not accept the fact that Kim was not an all-A student. Since I had developed a relationship with her, I knew that I could push Mrs. Jasper a little. I shared with her that I was not at all gifted in math, but it did not prevent me from getting a master's degree. I asked her about her education, and I discovered that her mother had treated her the way she was treating Kim, which is often the case. I tried to make her see that adding pressure to Kim at this time in her life was not a good idea. Her expectations of perfection could cause behavior problems in Kim. I hoped that she listened to me.

Another sensitive area is the parents' comparison of siblings. This is a major problem in many families. Children are already sensitive to whether their siblings are favored by their parents. Siblings know among themselves who has what talent and how each is treated. The worst thing a parent can say to a child is, "Why aren't you more like your brother or sister?" This is devastating to a child, because the child knows he cannot be like his brother or sister or that he is unique and cannot be a clone. When parents talk like this to their children, the children become angry, defensive, and hurt. Their self-esteem is lowered tremendously because they feel less than worthy in their parents' eyes.

If Johnny gets As in school, and Tommy gets Bs and Cs with the same amount of effort, Tommy already feels that his brother is smarter than he is. He doesn't need his parents to remind him. As mentioned earlier, the important thought is that the world needs all kinds of people. The highly academic people may become doctors and lawyers, which we need. People who are mechanical and not academic become fixers of things, which we need. People who are very social and not highly academic become service providers, which we need. People who are physical and need to move around a lot may deliver our mail and build our houses, which we need. There is a place and an occupation for all people and for all skills. And we need them all for our society to work.

So, the bottom line is to accept your children for whoever they are. Accept their personalities and abilities. Accept them for being more or for being less. Help them to be successful and to find a place for themselves in life. Make them feel as if in your eyes they are the greatest! Love them.

Chapter 21

Reflections of Ninth Graders about Middle School

I went into some ninth-grade classes and asked the students to think back to middle school. What did they like and dislike? What do they remember? What were their experiences in middle school?

Interestingly, much of the conversation revolved around teachers. Elementary school teachers are supposed to be child-centered. This means that they want the child to be successful and build self-esteem. Having one teacher makes it easier to get in homework because that teacher reminds you at the end of the day what the work is. Also, parents of elementary school children are often involved with the school and keep in contact with the teacher. There is a natural support system of school and family that surrounds the child.

Middle school is different. Not only do students have seven teachers, but now each teacher has around 150 students. The focus on the curriculum starts to change. Teachers may show some impatience if work is not done. In addition, there are many more discipline problems in the classroom, which add stress to the teacher's day. Thus, the student-teacher relationship changes. This is a major adjustment for middle school children, because they will never again have the kind of small, supportive environment that they had in elementary school. However, by the time they get to high school, they get used to the routine.

So this is why ninth graders have such strong feelings about their middle school teachers. They liked some of their teachers, and they hated others. They felt negatively about the ones they disliked for many reasons. Perhaps the teacher went too fast or was too loud. Sometimes a teacher would make a reference to being a "slacker," or having lazy habits. Moreover, if a student dislikes a teacher, that student most likely will slack off on the work. Students in middle school often align their feelings about their teachers with the amount of work they will do: "I remember Ms. Smith. She was very strict, and I didn't like that. That's why I failed her class. It was her fault."

However, some teachers were very popular. These teachers seemed to care a lot about the students, and they had a sense of humor and were patient but also maintained classroom control. One student recalled a popular math teacher in sixth grade. He received lots of gifts at winter break, and on his birthday a group of girls decorated his room and brought a cake in. He gave his students extra chances, and they appreciated that. He was always willing to give help during lunch. If an honors group did poorly on a test, he would allow the girls and boys to study more, and then he would retest them.

Sometimes children misinterpret a teacher's motives. If a teacher admonishes the class for talking too much, a student may think that the teacher is being "mean" to him or her. It is important, therefore, to find out how your middle school child feels about his or her teachers. If your child has negative feelings, it would be good to have a conference so that the teacher could reassure the student that he or she was not disliked.

Mrs. Jerome called me because Glen said that his math teacher didn't like him. When she asked why, Glen couldn't give a lot of reasons. She "yelled" at him (this usually means asking him to correct his behavior), and she didn't call on him when he raised his hand. I told Mrs. Jerome that the teacher, Glen, and I would have a conference. When I told the teacher about Glen's feelings, she was surprised. She was a strict teacher, and she liked to keep the class moving. But she expected students to misbehave sometimes, and she really didn't dislike anyone. After all, this is what a teacher had to live with every day. So, we had a conference, and the teacher told Glen that she thought that he was very capable and that when she disciplined the class, he should not take it personally. She would also try to call on Glen more often. Mrs. Jerome called after the conference to say that the meeting really helped Glen, and his attitude had changed.

The students that I interviewed also talked a lot about their behavior. Some of them thought that it was fun to get in trouble. Being sent to the office when it was busy was entertaining. The boys liked to play fight and punch each other a lot. They resented the fact that the administrators were constantly getting into their business. However, they admitted that strong consequences made them control themselves some of the time. It was clear from these interviews that their age brought out a lot of impulsive behavior, and when they crossed the line it was important for adults to intervene. Some of the students especially loved eighth grade because of the power that they had. They liked walking through the halls and watching the sixth graders get out of their paths. It is important for middle schools to be sure that eighth-grade classes are not near the sixth graders.

Lunch was clearly the highlight of the day. The students loved socializing, and they liked the noisy environment. They even enjoyed the new variety of foods offered to them. In many schools, seats are assigned in the lunchroom after students decide whom they want to sit with. But this can become a problem, especially with the girls, because their friendships can change rapidly. In addition, girls can develop misunderstandings, which cause love/hate relationships. If a girl is not talking to the person that she is sitting next to, because someone told her that that person revealed some personal information about her, then she has a problem. Also, there are some students who are unique. They don't fit in with the others, and they sometimes can't find a table to accept them. As a solution, it is a good idea for schools to allow some children to eat their lunch in a classroom that is monitored by a teacher. This would allow the shy children, and also those who are different or who are teased a lot, to find a quieter, more accepting environment.

Jeff was very artistic and intelligent. He also came from a family where many members had emotional problems. Jeff had an anxiety disorder, and he was also very short. In middle school a boy like that is often teased. When he grows up, Jeff can get a great job using his artistic talent. But I had to work with him a great deal to convince him not to draw negative attention to himself. He liked to come to my office to each lunch often, and we would talk.

The students said that being teased depended a lot on whom they hung out with. If they tried to be with the popular kids, they were teased less. If someone stayed alone and appeared vulnerable, then he or she would be teased more. In other words, you would be "cool" by association. Clearly, the main word that boys use to denigrate others is "fag." This is all too common in schools. It's amazing! It is no wonder that homosexual teens are so vulnerable to depression and suicide in high school. As for sexual harassment by boys of girls, one girl said, "That's what boys do—talk about girls' bodies." Because this is so pervasive, they don't even recognize that it is sexual harassment. Name-calling and insults are much too common in schools. Teachers should be sensitive to this and stop it when they hear it.

Many of the students talked about how difficult it was to pay attention. They had gone from elementary school, which had a lot of activities and lessons structured throughout the day, to a seven-period day of classes that are fifty minutes in length. Or, some have block scheduling, where classes are about one and one-half hours long, and they do not have the same classes every day. Because this "entertainment" generation is used to changing their focus often, concentrating for forty minutes becomes "boring." This is another problem with which middle school teachers have to deal. By the time they get to high school, the students are used to listening for longer periods of time. It is the middle school teachers who have to "break them in," allowing them to experience extended periods of time listening.

I remember how Mrs. Sorringer, the sixth-grade social studies teacher, told me that her students so often looked bored or restless. I suggested that she break up the forty-five-minute teaching time into several segments. It is a good idea to change activities every fifteen minutes if you can do that. She decided that each day she would have a time for the lecture, for group work and for bookwork, and for starting homework. It made the class better for her, too.

What the students loved most was the opportunity to make new friends. Being highly socialized as most students are today, it was fun to meet people from another elementary school and expand friendships. Then, they could go home and monopolize the telephone all night connecting with their new friends. Again, it is important for parents to find out who these new friends are and to invite them over, so they can meet them and connect with their parents.

One of the best suggestions came at the end of my discussion. One student said that it would be really helpful if schools could have a two-week orientation session over the summer so that incoming sixth graders could get to know the school and start to make new friends. They said that arriving for the first day of sixth grade, never having been there, was very frightening. Many schools have a two-day summer program, but the students felt that it was not enough. For sixth graders, just getting the feel of a middle school, which is structurally very different from elementary, is a major adjustment.

Overall, the students expressed a lot of feelings. I would guess that many of them never expressed their feelings about their middle school experiences to their parents. I would therefore suggest that parents use those good communication skills to make their children feel comfortable talking to them and sharing their day. Often, just talking helps a person feel better.

Chapter 22

The Effects of Divorce on Middle School Children

The definition of the word "family" has changed dramatically in the past decade. The traditional "nuclear" family, consisting of two parents and their children, has given way to the "extended" family, which includes multigenerations of people close to the family who participate in raising children, "single-parent" families, and "blended" families, which include stepparents and stepchildren. The acceptance of divorce in our society, and the increasingly large numbers of divorce, has helped to create new definitions of family.

The trauma of divorce affects every member of the family to some degree. The major difficulty that divorce brings to children is a dramatic change in family life as they have known it. There are various problems that children grapple with: a change in economic status; visitation, or lack thereof, with the absent parent; a shifting of responsibilities onto children; adjustment problems of parents themselves; a change in residence; a lack of understanding of why their lives have changed; negative feelings which they do not know how to deal with; and social changes due to all of the conditions just listed. These and other problems can result in major adjustment problems that have impact on school activities and cause a negative effect on a child's achievement. When children come to school upset, angry, confused, and unfocused, you can imagine how their class work can suffer.

The first year following divorce is the most difficult one for children (Thomas S. Parish and Stanley E. Wigle, 1985). They usually stay with the mother. Children are greatly affected by the absence of the father, whether or not there is continued involvement by him; the adjustment process of the mother; and the degree of hostility between the parents. The more strained the above relationships are, the more harm that is done to the children, especially boys, who often fare worse than girls (Carin Rubinstein, 1980). Children who spend little time with their parents after the breakup are more likely to develop emotional problems, including depression. In addition, the economic loss can cause great trauma. Having less money to spend and feeling different from their peers is very depressing to children, and it makes them angry. Some mothers have to work two jobs, which makes them less accessible to their children. Many children of divorced parents are alone a lot, unmonitored, and feeling unhappy. There may be less parental nurturing and inconsistent discipline in the home.

Divorce can cause a laundry list of negative feelings among children. They feel sad at the breakup of the family unit, guilt over fantasized or actual bad behavior that they think contributed to the separation, worry over distressed parents, anger at the parents for the disruption, shame about the breakup, and a great sense of loneliness. The anger is manifested in negative and aggressive behavior toward parents as well as teachers and classmates. Symptoms of depression can include absent-mindedness, nervousness, fatigue, moodiness, declining grades, acting-out behaviors, and physical complaints. Worried children can have a short attention span.

Children whose parents divorce usually move through the grief stages of denial, anger, guilt, depression, and acceptance, which can take two to three years to complete (Jeff Grimes, 1982). Children grieve for the loss of the total family relationship, and they need much emotional support. There can be feelings of powerlessness and a loss of control, which create a negative self-concept and a feeling of being overburdened. The anxiety and hostility that they feel can cause acting-out behaviors or withdrawal. While children need support, parents are often caught up in their own major adjustment problems, leaving little time and energy to help their children.

There can be different kinds of problems that spring from the troubled feelings that children experience. Getting in trouble and acting out can be a result of defensive coping behaviors, because children can feel overwhelmed. Children from single-parent families represent the largest percentages of tardiness, truancy, dropouts, and expulsions. There can also be more risk-taking behaviors, including sexual promiscuity and drug and alcohol abuse. When fathers abandon girls, these girls may seek male approval through early sexual behaviors. They are also at risk of developing eating disorders, and their self-esteem plummets (Judith S. Wallerstein and Joan B. Kelly, 1980). Children of divorce often feel a loss of control, which causes a feeling of powerlessness in terms of decision-making and coping.

Children seldom continue to do well in school during and immediately after a divorce. Many parents and teachers expect children to function well in school despite turmoil at home. Children are desperately trying to cope with an ambiguous situation and are afraid of losing the parent that is leaving. Children may have tremendous problems concentrating in school and doing their work because of the emotions that flood their minds and cause uncertainty. Many single parents are less involved with their child's schoolwork because the parent feels overwhelmed. There is a definite link between parental interest and self-esteem. If a parent spends less time with his or her children, there is a perception of a lowering parental interest, support, and participation (Doren J. Walker, 1993). Children are aware of being manipulated by parents who have power battles and denigrate each other, which makes children resentful of more powerful external forces, including adults at school. The child's value system and role models become blurred, weakening the child's ego.

Fathers who abandon sons cause a tremendous amount of harm. A boy gets his male identity from his father. If his father is lazy, mean, irresponsible, and abusive, then a son may feel that he also is a bad and worthless person. This causes tremendous anger in boys, who will then turn their anger outward or inward. If it is outward, they will get into trouble in school. If it is inward, it becomes depression and a shutting down of normal functioning. In situations like this, it is important for a mother to connect to male family members or friends so that the son can have positive male role models. The Big Brother programs can also be of tremendous help.

What can parents do to help their children during this difficult time of change? First, a parent should always call the school counselor and ask him or her to inform the teachers that the child is going through a divorce in the family. When teachers know of such a circumstance, they will often be more patient and understanding. The single parent should ask the counselor to keep her informed of her child's progress on a periodic basis. Also, the parent should ask the counselor if there is a divorce group in school that the child can join. Group counseling is especially helpful to children starting in early adolescence. Meeting once a week for at least two months in a group with other children who are experiencing a divorce in the family can be helpful in several ways. It is reassuring for children to know that others are experiencing the same problems and have the same feelings. Just expressing their feelings is helpful. Additionally, the members of the group can help each other as they learn to solve problems and communicate in a different way with their parents.

Parents should never speak critically of the other parent. This makes children feel so sad because the child really loves both parents. Never put the child in the middle as a message carrier or decision-maker. Don't pump a child for information about the other parent. This too hurts the child because it is asking him or her to break a confidence with someone who is loved. It is best not to discuss finances with the child because that adds unfair stress. It is very helpful to have routines that are dependable so that a child can feel stability even with the change. But parents also need to be flexible, because their lives become more complex. When a noncustodial parent cancels and changes plans often, the message given to the child is that he or she is not important to the parent. Parents shouldn't forget that they too need counseling when they are going through a painful divorce, as well as the children.

Try to keep the child's best interests in mind. Consider what the child's feelings and desires are. Ask your child how he or she is feeling, how school is, how the adjustment process is going. Assure your child that you love him or her, and that the child was not the cause of the divorce. Encourage your child to spend time with the noncustodial parent, because that will help your child. Don't shuffle your child around a lot to other people. Remember that a child of a divorce is never certain whether he or she is loved. Let your actions prove that you care. And don't make your child your confidant, asking for opinions. Use your friends for help so that you can help your child.

Although a parent who is single often feels lonely, it is really best not to try to build a social life soon. When a single mom starts dating, and she brings different men into her children's lives, she can give the message that a man is more important to her than her children. If you get divorced, learn to live with some loneliness for a while. When a mom dates a new man for several months, and they involve the children in their activities, those children start to become attached to the new man. If he leaves, then the children feel further abandonment. It is better for a single mom to build her life around her children for a while. Going to work, going to counseling to understand why the marriage broke up, and taking care of children is enough to fill anyone's time.

Most children eventually adjust to divorce, and many are able to emerge intact from the experience. Others feel as though their lives have been broken, and they may have a difficult time trusting in romantic relationships when they get older. If children feel that both parents love them and are involved in their lives, they will have the best opportunity to adjust well. If the routines of children can stay fairly consistent and predictable, they can learn to trust again. It will take dedication and maturity on the part of both parents to help their children adjust to divorce.

Chapter 23

Stepparenting Can Work—Or It Can Be a Disaster

A natural and common step after divorce is remarriage. Most people who divorce feel very lonely, and they long for a better relationship. Although children can fill their lives, they do not replace a mate. Thus, with the high rate of divorce, there is also a high rate of second marriages. These marriages have so many players—his children, her children, ex-spouses, grandparents, and others—that the roles often become ambiguous and conflicted. The key factor contributing to a second divorce is children. Parents need to understand the feelings, manipulations, and complications involved in stepparenting. The adults also need to understand their own feelings about their children and their spouse's children. Here are some important suggestions, routines, and rules that will help a newly blended family to become relatively harmonious. Without this information, parents are liable to find chaos overwhelming them. If you thought that parenting was difficult, you will find that stepparenting is like a roller coaster ride, and you'd better hang on tightly.

Probably the most critical adjustment involves the feelings that parents have toward stepchildren and vice versa. The reality is that we love and favor our own children. We may also love another adult, but his or her children are often felt as encumbrances to us: they are offspring to be tolerated. Because we naturally love our own children, we are far more tolerant and patient with them. Moreover, we are often in denial about the problems that our children have and how we may contribute to them. We feel an affinity for our children. We are often physically affectionate with our children. We know them so well, and we may cater to their tastes and desires. We are comfortable with their personality traits, even though they may be difficult to live with. The known is what we are used to. The unknown is not comfortable.

So, here are stepchildren suddenly jumping into our lives. We want to be nice to them, but we do not automatically love them. They certainly do not automatically love us. In fact, they may dislike and resent us. It takes time to get to know others. It takes time for familiarity and comfort to develop. It takes a lot of time to adjust to new living circumstances. But we are not a patient society. We are used to instant-on TV, microwave ovens, and automatic teller machines. Human relationships don't work that way.

So, the very first quality that we must develop is patience. We must also have realistic expectations. We must first temper our feelings about our stepchildren. Deep down, we may wish they did not exist. When we marry a second time, we are marrying a package deal: our spouse and the accompanying children and family. A stepparent has to be ultrasensitive to family dynamics. For example, his children may be jealous when he pays attention to her, and her children may be jealous when she pays attention to him. We have to expect stepchildren to act on their feelings of jealousy. We must be patient and try to find a way to minimize those feelings. The children will act like children. The adults should behave in a more mature manner and monitor their own feelings of jealousy to help the children to adjust.

Mrs. Miller called to ask if I had any suggestions for her about mealtime. She had been remarried for two months, and the dinner hour was a mess. While she was making dinner, her husband would come home from work, give her a kiss, and ask about her day. At about the same time, her son and daughter would start fighting. Her new husband would lose patience and yell that he did not want to come home to fighting. What could she do? She saw the jealousies in all of them, and she also loved them and wanted this marriage to work. I suggested that she ask her children to help her nightly with dinner. Then, when her husband came home, the first people that he would greet would be her children, not her. They would then feel that they were important to him, which would reduce their need to fight in order to get attention. He could save his warm greetings for his wife at the end of his conversation with his stepchildren. Mrs. Miller liked these ideas. I invited her to call me back with any other problems. I knew that there would be more, and I knew that strategies could help.

Second-marriage families have so many issues to deal with: both small and large. Parts of the daily routine can often become roadblocks: household chores, eating preferences and habits, the remote control. These need to be defined, taking everyone's needs into consideration. For example, during a period of divorce, children become used to changes in dinner and TV watching. The children often dictate their desires in these areas because a single mother feels hassled and busy, and she often gives in to the children.

Enter a new husband. He has his eating preferences. He also may be used to controlling the remote, but the children also may like to control what shows they watch. He wants the house kept a certain way, perhaps different from what the children are accustomed to. What should be done? We can only fall back on communication and compromise. Because children suffer tremendously from divorce, the adults should probably consider the children's needs and desires above those of the parents. Certainly, there should be compromise. But if the children are used to certain dinners, and a stepparent wants to make changes, those changes should be made slowly. Let the entire family plan the meals for the week. Decide what television programs are most important to everyone and take turns choosing. Develop a spirit of inclusiveness.

In stepfamilies, there are always those lurking in the shadows, the ex-parent, the ex-grandparents and other ex-families, and friends. The hard fact about divorce is that the biological parents will always have to discuss issues and events. These parents must try to get along for the sake of the sanity of the children. There will be school issues, health problems, money problems, and decisions about holidays and vacations, let alone future graduations and marriages. If parents cannot talk and they cannot change patterns of communication where they level blame and yell at each other, the children will be miserable, and the new spouses will be often irritated. If there is a problem in school, the school staff must convince both parents to talk to the child to help to change the inappropriate behavior. If parents cannot talk to each other, how are they going to help the child effectively? If a grandparent is asking for extra time with the children, which affects the visitation of the ex-spouse, how can that be resolved if the parents cannot talk to each other in a civil manner? Most people end a marriage with feelings of anger and resentment. These feelings need to be put aside for the benefit of the children, the number one priority.

I had to call Mrs. Miller back. Her son Ben was developing a problem completing his homework. Ben told me that when he visited his father during the week, his father would often have plans to go bowling. His father would tell Ben that he could finish his homework when he got home, but that was often too close to bedtime. I told Mrs. Miller that I would call Ben's dad and suggest that he have a complete list of Ben's homework assignments when he saw his son. Then he would be sure that the homework would be done before they went bowling. I asked Mrs. Miller to be sure that Ben have this list when his father picked him up. This way, both parents would help Ben to complete his homework on those visitation nights.

Visitation schedules are often a source for arguments. It is very, very critical that parents develop a reasonable schedule, and then follow it consistently and faithfully. Children whose noncustodial parent (usually the father) does not provide consistency usually feel very bad about changes. For example, if a father cannot have dinner on Tuesday as he usually does, and this happens often, the child will feel that he or she is not very important to the father. Fathers who are erratic and often change plans actually damage their children's self-esteem. When a parent is consistent and dependable, the child's trust is renewed. When a child is in middle school, the life of the child can become more complex because of various activities, such as sports, the child may engage in. When that happens, parents should be flexible in following the child's schedule, because these activities are so important to the child.

Mrs. Miller called to say she was having a problem with her ex-husband because Ben started spring soccer practice on Tuesdays and Thursdays, and practice sometimes ran late when Mr. Miller came to pick him up for dinner. Mrs. Miller was frustrated, and she was worried about the impact of this on his homework. I suggested that she begin a time-management plan for those days. Ben should do his homework immediately after school, with no TV on those days. Then, if he was late for dinner, it would not be important because he would have the rest of the evening with his dad. I told Mrs. Miller that I would speak to Ben about this and send home a time management grid with him.

One of the most important rules about divorce is for all adults to refrain from speaking badly of the other adults. It is so easy to add frustration to anger and to denigrate an ex-spouse or a newly married spouse. These comments are extremely hurtful to children, and they make children feel as if they have been put in the middle. It's hard enough for a child to get used to a stepparent without the custodial parent saying negative things about him or her. It's also very important for mothers to refrain from criticizing a boy's father, because a boy often develops his self-image from that of his father. If a father is undependable and of little worth, then a boy may subconsciously think he is also. Even if a father acts undependably, a mother should just ignore this and stress how great it is that a boy's dad is an important part of his life.

If money issues are a major problem in a first marriage, they can become even more of a problem in a second. When you combine support payments, a mother's salary, and a father's salary plus his support payments, you have a beehive to wade through. And, of course, parents still have the inclination to favor their natural children. The only way to resolve money issues, as with every problem, is to talk about it and work toward compromise.

It was Mrs. Miller again. She had two of her own children, and her new husband also had two. A problem was developing over presents given for the winter holiday. Mrs. Miller was used to being very generous with her children, but she did not want to spend as much money on her stepchildren. I suggested to her that having a harmonious blended family was more important at this time. I felt that she should set a precedent of spending the same amount on each of the four children. The children would appreciate that treating everyone equally was the rule, and this would help each of the stepchildren to accept each other. Mrs. Miller's children already knew that she loved them. Forming a new, cohesive family was more important.

Discipline is another serious issue. It is important that the biological parent do the majority of the disciplining. When a new stepparent tries to discipline, a child will probably feel as if this new adult has no right to tell him or her what to do or not do. When this happens, the child and the new parent develop an enormous amount of animosity over punishment. A child feels that only a natural parent has the right to discipline. This doesn't mean that a stepparent should not express views and have values. But if real punishment is necessary, the biological parent should give it.

There are always going to be some issues, problems, and feelings to deal with. Stepfamilies should have weekly meetings to iron these things out. If problems persist, they should seek family therapy to help them. Everyone needs to develop empathy and to try to see the others' points of view. Recognize that it takes time for people to adjust to new living circumstances. And, most importantly, everyone should try to treat each other with respect and consideration. Parents should always make all of the children feel that they are loved and valued.

Chapter 24

The Importance of Early and Continuous Career Exploration

The world of work has changed dramatically and is continuing to do so. At one time, children followed into the same occupation as their parents, and parents often worked at the same job and for the same employer until they retired. For example, a carpenter would train his son to be ready for an apprenticeship at eighteen. The son of a lawyer often went into law. Family businesses were always handed down to the children. Women were basically homemakers until the 1960s. At that time, large numbers of females went to college, but the basic majors were limited to teaching and nursing.

Now our life is very different. Women are lawyers and doctors and carpenters. Children usually pursue their own career interests, often different from that of their parents. All careers are open to all people today if they have the interest and the desire to train. Jobs are also changing rapidly. Jobs will exist in twenty years that are not in existence today. Instead of very specific training, students are told today that the development of skills is important. Yet, what leads us to specific occupations are our interest, ability, and experience. The earlier that parents can help their children to understand how their specific uniqueness can translate into a career, the easier it will be for children to see themselves in a future occupation. When children develop a desire to pursue a career from the age of middle school on, they become more serious about their education. They become better students because they have developed a goal for themselves. It is important for parents to be aware of career information.

All students today will need an education beyond high school if they are going to have meaningful careers. There are many choices here. Community colleges offer two-year programs granting an associate degree. These are possible occupations:

- computer technician
- surveyor
- dental hygienist
- medical laboratory technician
- commercial artist
- hotel/restaurant manager
- engineering technician
- automotive mechanic
- administrative assistant
- plant operator
- heating/air conditioning technician

There are also technical institutes that train people for mechanical jobs.

Of course, four-year colleges or universities grant bachelor's degrees. One can become a teacher, accountant, engineer, journalist, pharmacist, computer systems analyst, dietitian, graphic designer, public relations specialist, and more. More than four years are required to become a lawyer, doctor, professor, psychologist, and veterinarian, among others.

Planning for the right college courses starts in middle school. By the time a child starts middle school, families should begin talking about college. Parents should stress the need for further education after high school and planning how to get there. Everyone knows that good high school grades and the right courses are important for admission to college, along with SAT, or Scholastic Aptitude Test, scores. But it is important to understand that a college education also builds on the knowledge and skills acquired in earlier years. Research shows that students who take algebra and geometry by the end of eighth and ninth grades are more likely to go to college than students who do not. It is important to take algebra in middle school so that students can enroll in higher math and science classes in high school. Children should always be challenged to reach academically by taking one or more honors classes. It is natural for children to want to do less work, but it is important for parents to recognize this and set high standards.

After choosing the middle school courses to prepare for college, parents should then begin to analyze their individual children for possible career direction and also to teach them about occupations and the world of work. There are many career theorists who have analyzed information about careers. All work can be divided into four entities: dealing with data (such as numbers and organizing things); dealing with things (such as goods and instruments); working with ideas (such as concepts and information); and working with people. One's job can be strictly in one of these areas, such as fixing computers (working with things), or one can combine areas, such as working with people and data, as in marketing and sales.

So, the first thing to do is to analyze your children's personalities and interests as they relate to the above information. For example, a child who is very good at math and at spatial relations (putting things together) at an early age may grow up to be an accountant or an architect. Parents should point out to children what they are good at and how that may transfer into future careers. If a child is an introvert, that is, he or she prefers to be alone a good deal of the time, that child should not be directed into a social occupation such as teaching or law. A child who is an extrovert, or one who enjoys being with people much of the time, should not be directed to an occupation that has little interaction with people, such as a computer programmer. Look at your children's personalities, abilities, interests, and experiences for career direction. This doesn't mean that anything is set in stone at an early age. What it means is that you are teaching your children to look at themselves, to understand and evaluate themselves, and to be thinking about future careers (see Figure 24.1).

Then teach your children about the world of work. There are many factors to consider. Some people love to be outside most of the time. There are careers that would place them there, such as working for the government in national parks. Some people like the security of a nine-to-five job, while others like to have changes in routine. Some want to work for others to guarantee a basic salary, while others enjoy being an entrepreneur and seeing what their abilities and effort can bring them. Some people like to read and think a lot, while others need to move around. All of these and other factors comprise the world of work, and we all have personalities and bodies that feel more comfortable in one setting or another.

As a parent, you can help your children to understand themselves and the kind of environment in which they would be comfortable. For example, a person who has ADD, or attention deficit disorder, should be in an occupation where he or she can move around and have changes throughout the day, whereas a child who is capable of focusing for long periods of time could be an accountant or a computer programmer. I have a student whose entire family loves boating, and they spend a good deal of the summer on the water. This child already knows that he wants to be in the Coast Guard. I have another student who has been cooking since the age of eight, and he wants to go to a culinary institute and

Figure 24.1
Career Analysis

Parents should explore this with their children and have many conversations about future careers.

Name:_____

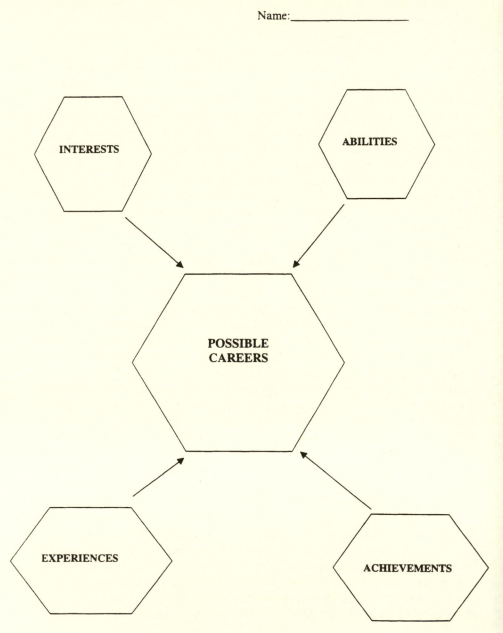

become a chef. Yet another student is an avid reader and loves to watch programs about the law on television. She may well become a lawyer. Some children reveal very dominant interests at an early age, but many do not. I have spoken to so many boys who want to be professional athletes. I always tell them that they must have another occupation to fall back on. If they are so enamored of sports, they can become physical education teachers.

Children in middle school should understand that all of the education they are receiving is important because it trains them to think, write, analyze, infer, gather data, do math and get along with others and work in groups, among other things. These skills take years to develop, and middle school is important because children are being challenged by higher-level material in their classes. Sometimes their class work might be particularly interesting, and this can then become a direction for a career path. For example, the science curriculum in seventh grade may study the systems of the body, which could spark an interest in medicine. Or a unit in English class could require reading from the newspaper, and a child could become very interested in journalism. Exposure in elective courses such as art and music can guide a child to a future career. All experiences in school, and enrichment experiences outside of school, can introduce a child to a possible future career.

It is important for parents to know that there are many different ways to assess career potentials. These assessments can be done on paper, or there are computer programs that are very effective. Basically, they ask a person to choose between many sets of activities, such as: Would you rather attend a small party or a large party? Would you rather work a machine or talk to a person? These sets of questions then come together to give a final breakdown of possible occupations. In my school, we do a computer career assessment in seventh grade, and each child has a printout suggesting careers of interest. This computer program also has a career exploration component where a child can look at specific fields and find out about training requirements, salary schedules, what the work is, and so on. Another way is to go to professional career specialist psychologists for help in selecting a field. But middle school is a good place to start with the simpler career assessments to help children to become interested in thinking about their futures.

Finally, it is also important for parents to think about financing a college education as early as possible. There are public (state) and private universities, and they are all expensive. Costs include tuition and fees, books, room and board (if one is living away from home), and expenses. State universities are less expensive than private ones. In addition to families saving for college, a student can seek loans, grants, and scholarships. Much of this information is now available on the Internet. To get an idea of how much expenses are now for major colleges in the

United States, visit http://www.finaid.org/. Even though college is expensive, it is important to remember that the average salary of a person with a college education is higher than that of a person without one.

So, middle school is an important time to introduce your children to career and college information. If they know that you have high expectations for achievement, but you also accept their strengths and weaknesses while you guide them to possible careers, they will feel secure about their future.

Chapter 25

After Middle School—High School Is Different

Once your child has made it through eighth grade, another major transition occurs: going to high school. There are many new adjustments to be made. However, it is usually easier for a fourteen-year-old to adjust than it is for an eleven-year-old. But parents need to be aware of the changes involved, because even though they are bigger, teenagers are still children. Although teens tend to become very private about their lives, it is still very important for parents to remain involved and knowledgeable about their children's activities. Often, the teens who bring weapons to school are those who feel estranged from the world and do not connect with their parents. It is also necessary for parents to know what is in their children's rooms and to be aware of their activities and their attitudes.

The first thing that a student may notice about high school is that it is much larger than middle school, perhaps even more than twice the size. The high schools in the area where I live have approximately 2,000 students in them. Obviously, the larger the size, the more impersonal a school can feel to a student. Most students love the increased freedom because they can go from one class to another without the supervision they had in middle school. This occurs at a time when teens are becoming independent, breaking away from the family, and they welcome the autonomy that they now have over their day.

Another change is that the academic situation is much different in high school. Now there are credit and graduation requirements. It often takes ninth graders a while to understand this, because middle school does not have requirements but, instead, a more flexible design. If a student fails a course in high school, that course has to be retaken in night school or summer school, at the family's expense. Many states have final exam requirements that affect a semester grade. Some stipulate that if a final exam is failed, then the course is failed. There may also be attendance requirements that, if abused, can lead to a loss of credit in a course. In addition, students may have as many as fourteen teachers a year, because at the semester change a student may have different teachers. The kind of rapid adjustment to different teachers prepares teens for college, where every class has a different professor and possibly a different building.

The courses your child chooses in high school are very important. Colleges are looking for students who have undertaken a rigorous academic program and have taken honors and advanced placement courses. Most colleges require two years of a foreign language. Parents need to know what courses their children are taking to be sure they have made selections that will help them to get into colleges. Honors and advanced placement classes give additional weighted points to the grade point average. The high-achieving students who take a full load of high-level classes can earn more than a 4.0 grade point average, which makes them eligible for more demanding colleges. Advanced placement classes offer the opportunity to earn college credit if a certain score is achieved on the advanced placement (AP) exam.

Parents must understand that high school teachers will not be calling them as often as teachers did in elementary and middle school. High school teachers focus on their curriculum and on preparation for the final exams. The teachers certainly form relationships with their students and encourage them to do well, and most schools have some kind of interim notice system that is mailed home so that parents can know if a child is in danger of failing a subject. But the assumption in high school is that a teen is more independent and is taking charge of his or her life. A parent should not assume that if a call is not made that a student is doing well. Of course, parents are always welcome to call teachers and make inquiries.

Meanwhile, there are more social changes that occur in high school. Now one can choose friends from hundreds of students in different grades. What usually happens is that teens make friends with others who have the same interests and attitudes, be they positive or negative. The athletes, the musicians, the artists, the popular kids, the computer kids, and the unhappy kids all find each other. This is a natural separation, and it's fine, of course, except in the case of the kids with many problems. Teens who are not achieving and who have home problems are often very negative. These are the ones who are at risk of cutting school and experimenting with alcohol and drugs. Teachers will often point out these kids to counselors, who then try to help. But an angry teen is difficult to work with. When home problems have become insurmountable, some young people get lost. That's why it is so important for parents to know who the friends of their children are.

There are many positive things in a teen's life. High school has a wealth of after-school activities that are lots of fun, such as building floats for a homecoming dance, or joining groups such as SADD (Students Against Drunk Driving) or groups that enter debate contests or theater groups. And, of course, there are the football and basketball games. These are exciting social events for teens. Adolescents also look forward to driving and getting part-time jobs to help pay for the insurance. Dating relationships often begin in high school. This is an area that parents need to watch because of the possibility of sexual relationships and their consequences. Teens can seriously fall in love. Their hormones are raging. And a breakup of a romantic relationship can cause terrible heartache and actually precipitate a suicide attempt. This is serious business.

Applying for college is both an exciting and stressful experience. Sixteen seems to be a magical age for teenagers. It is a point of maturity. The difference between a fourteen- and a sixteen-year-old is monumental. Ninth graders are like reheated eighth graders. Eleventh grade marks a real change, which is good, because that is the time when teens should begin their search for further education. Whether it is a four-year college, a two-year college, a training school, or an apprenticeship, additional schooling is necessary because a high school diploma may not be enough to enter a chosen career with. Again, teens need the help of their parents in searching for information and making a decision. Senior year is very stressful because of the deadlines that colleges have for their applications.

Meanwhile, high school can be a very positive or a negative time for teenagers. For those for whom it is negative, emotional problems can take a turn for the worst. The eating disorders or depression that can start in middle school can become full-blown problems in high school, needing a lot of professional intervention. The risk of suicide for teens is high. The fact that most high school students start experimenting with alcohol use can increase this danger. No matter how well you try to monitor your teen, there are going to be exposures to alcohol and drugs. Teens driving in crowded cars are also in a risky position. There are a lot of automobile accidents among teenagers, and, the more friends that they have in a car, the higher the risk for an accident. Parents have to be very firm about setting rules about driving, about knowing where their teens are, whom they are with, when they will be home, and having phone numbers to reach them. Some teens may resist these rules. If they resist a lot, that could be a sign of a problem.

So, high school opens up a big, new, varied, and exciting world. Navigating it is not easy for all teens. When you compare high school with middle school, certainly the problems of middle school look smaller. But with each age and at each stage, the challenges of parenting are huge and require time, commitment, and energy. A devoted parent will reap incredible rewards when the children are grown and are happy, functioning adults who still keep in contact with them.

Chapter 26

Resilience

We are all born with an innate capacity for resilience: enduring, snapping back, and dealing positively with life's difficulties. Resilience helps us to develop many skills throughout life. Children develop social competence when they learn social behaviors in school and in activities. They learn problem-solving skills when adults discuss problems and solutions. Independence and a sense of purpose also develop as children accept challenges and make decisions about their lives. Resilience is now being recognized as a foundation for drug and violence prevention and health promotion.

The focus of resilience is now shifting from the emphasis on negative factors in a child's life to the idea of primary prevention. What factors can enable children to develop resilience as they are growing up? What can schools and homes do to foster resilience in children?

Research shows that the link between protective factors in a child's environment and that child's healthy development and success is stronger than the link between risk factors and negative outcomes. This means that schools and families have tremendous power to develop resilience in children (Robert Brooks and Sam Goldstein, 2001).

Let us first examine what resilience is. One major quality is social competence. This is defined as being responsive to others, establishing positive relationships, and therefore getting positive treatment from others. In order to develop social competence, a child must have flexibility, empathy, communications skills, and a sense of humor.

At a team meeting, Chris's teachers expressed concern to me that he would treat his classmates in ways that would cause him to be rejected. He would make fun of others, occasionally hit someone, or take someone else's pencil. I knew that Chris was not developing social competence. I decided to start a "friends" counseling group of six to eight students where we would role-play positive social behaviors.

Another quality of resilience is resourcefulness, which is comprised of many traits. Having good decision-making skills develops from having good problem-solving skills, seeking help from others, and recognizing alternative ways to resolve conflict. Sometimes, a person just has to be strong during difficult times and then be able to relieve stress in a positive manner and to soothe one's self. This also includes the ability to recognize that you are enduring difficult circumstances in life and then to create strategies to make your life better.

I knew that Sharon was an unusual person. When she entered sixth grade, she liked to come and talk to me about her alcoholic mother. She had talked to her elementary school counselor a lot, and she found it helpful just to vent and sometimes to get suggestions on how to cope at home. Her ability to see herself as a separate person from the rest of her family helped her to set goals so that her future could be a good one. She was beginning to understand that she did not have to have the problems that her mother had. This insight would help her to be resilient.

Autonomy is the quality of acting independently and having a sense of one's own identity. People who have this trait have positive control over their lives and accept responsibility for their actions. They develop a belief that they can do things well because they evaluate themselves honestly, and therefore they can learn from their mistakes. They want to be independent, and they seek activities they are interested in. Along with autonomy, it is important for children to develop a sense of purpose. They must be able to set goals for themselves and to envision what their future might be. They should realize that education is extremely important and that it will lead them to many opportunities in life.

Henry was an amazing newcomer to middle school. He wanted to know what extracurricular activities were available and how he could join them. He was in band and he was also athletic. He was very organized and seemed to be able to manage a full life. He had such a strong sense of who he was. He nearly always did his homework, and he said that he definitely would go to college. He thought that he might want to be a lawyer. His ambition and high self-esteem were amazing.

There are specific family conditions that contribute to the development of resilience in children. Having a close bond with a primary caregiver during the first year of life is extremely important. This means that whoever is with the baby the most, usually the mother, should be there every day, constantly attending to the infant's needs. Children learn during the first year of life whether or not they can trust. Trust is developed when the baby is fed when hungry, changed when necessary, held often, and talked to a lot. If the primary caregiver does this every day, the child feels safe and develops trust. Having four or fewer children spaced more than two years apart enables parents to form this close bond with each infant, giving them a strong foundation of love.

Having extended family or neighbors who can be depended upon helps a young person to become resilient. These relatives or friends must have strong values and make themselves available to the child. This will help the child to develop a sense of security, knowing that adults can be relied upon for help. Children need to feel loved by the primary adults in their lives. It takes time and attention for adults to convey this love. Knowing that you are loved as a child helps you to become resilient later in life when people may not treat you well.

The Willard family had to struggle because Mrs. Willard had physical problems that sometimes overwhelmed her. She was lucky to have a sister who was willing to step in whenever necessary to help the children. "Aunt Alice" would call me whenever Mrs. Willard was having a problem to find out how James was doing. I would always get a report from the teachers, of course. I knew that when Aunt Alice called, Mrs. Willard could not. James was lucky to have such a terrific aunt. I knew that this would help to compensate for the family problems, and it would keep James on track.

Meanwhile, having structure and rules in the home from childhood through adolescence helps children to become resilient. Without this order, life can seem chaotic in a home. When discipline is not consistent, when there are no habits in the family, when rules can be broken with no consequences sometimes and strict consequences other times, children can develop anxiety and resentment because their world is not defined. They also emerge into adulthood not knowing how to create structure in their lives.

Another way to develop resilience—that is surprising to many—is to require that children be helpful in the family or community, in other words, do volunteer work. When children grow up believing that they should be helpful to others, they develop a sense of the world that goes beyond their own, narrow life. This allows a person to see that many people need help. It also enables a person to forget his or her troubles and concentrate on someone else's problems. When a person develops a life-long orientation to helping others, that person is often happier, because giving to others provides a reward in itself.

The Taylor family was amazing. I knew that Mr. and Mrs. Taylor had two of their own children, and they also had a foster child. They treated all of the children equally, and the foster child was doing well in school. Then I found out that the family went to a soup kitchen to volunteer every weekend. What an example they were setting! And their son Jacob was always helpful to others in school. I could see where he had developed the spirit of giving to others.

Besides family, how can schools help to develop resilience in children? There are many ways. One is for teachers to develop caring and supportive relationships that include trust, compassion, and respect. The presence of at least one caring person, someone who understands that even if a child's behavior is inappropriate, the child is reacting according to his or her needs and requires patient re-direction, provides support for healthy development and learning. Children and adults often mention a teacher who was influential in accepting and guiding them. This is why it is important for parents to work with the schools in helping children.

Parents and schools also need to have positive, high expectations of all students, establishing rules and specifying consequences that are followed through consistently. Parents should be honest about their children's misbehavior and cooperate when schools administer consequences. This helps children to develop self-control and self-discipline. Children must be encouraged to achieve and be provided support to do so. They must be required to show respect for others and themselves. They must be told that they possess all of the qualities required to be successful in life if they will call forth the abilities that are within them. Of course, parents need to provide a home environment that is caring, supportive and consistent.

It is essential for all adults who interact with children to understand how resilience is developed. Instilling these qualities in children is a major preventative action that will help children to resist drug and alcohol addiction, to survive the challenges of growing up, and to become strong, self-confident adults who can instill resilience into the next generation.

Chapter 27

The Power of Family Love

When people get married in their twenties, as many do, they are embarking on an adventure that will bring them happiness, sadness, challenges, and problems. Forming a family is a basic human instinct that comes without a rulebook or a guide. Making a marriage succeed requires diligence, understanding, determination, and empathy.

Making a family succeed requires even more work, understanding, and commitment. But the benefits of having a close, loving family are numerous. These include having better health, feeling more secure in all of our relationships, and having emotional support throughout our entire lives.

There is an old saying that we choose our friends, but we do not choose our relatives. There are many families where people do not get along, and close relationships are lost. Yet it is our family with whom we share the tapestry of our lives, and it is our family who should be the ones to drop everything in our hours of need.

I was surprised to receive the phone call from my sister Beth. She lived two states away, and sometimes we would be so busy that a few months would go by without a phone call. We were close as adults and always interested in each other. Beth called to say that her husband said he was leaving, and she was devastated. They had gone to counseling, but her husband did not want to make any changes to make things better. Then she discovered that he was having an affair. I knew what I had to do. I immediately called the airlines for a ticket, called my boss to say that I would be gone for a few days, and went to see her.

She was so relieved that I was coming. But that is what the family does when it does its best.

When children are in middle school, they can become very insecure and full of anxiety. They will let out their frustrations and anger at home because home is safe. But in school, children keep all of this inside so that they can appear confident. This is a time when parents can become so confused and upset at the changed behavior of their children that they now begin to give up on them. It is important to remember that this is a difficult time for young adolescents, and their behavior is not necessarily a sign of a bad person but, rather, a young adult who is grappling with more than he or she can handle. It is very important for parents to dig their heels in and not give up on their children. Adolescents will be moody, angry, and irresponsible. Parents must realize that this is one of the phases of growing up, and they should negotiate with their children. Most adolescents become adults who are loving and independent. Many parents of adult children can recall times when their children were so difficult to live with that holding onto the relationship took tremendous strength. Yet these adult children turned out to be successful people who were close to their families. Parents should *never* give up on their children!

I knew that my daughter Jamie was having a hard time at school. She had red hair and freckles, and she was often made fun of by the new kids in sixth grade. She would come home in a bad mood. I tried to work with her every day, talking about how unimportant the opinions of these kids were. I gave her lots of hugs and told her that I knew that this was difficult. I suggested that we make more arrangements with her good friends to make her feel better. I reminded her that she was a wonderful person and that I loved her very much. Even though I was tired after work, I put that aside to help my daughter. I wanted us to always have a good relationship, even though there would be rocky times.

It is the family unit that gives strength and resilience to our children. The family unit can be the traditional family, or it can be an extended family and the community. To help them feel secure, children need as many adults as possible in their lives. Family fun times and family traditions that are built into daily life help children to feel the love that they need. You really only have a relatively short time to be a parent, perhaps twenty years out of an eighty-plus-year lifespan. The more that you give now to your children in time, love, and energy, the more you will get back for the rest of your life. Each day gives us another opportunity to try again, to love again, to be positive again, and to reap the joy that can bring. There is a power in love to help our children, to guide and comfort them, and help them to grow up to be loving individuals who can contribute to the next generation.

Bibliography

Barovick, Harriet. "Reluctant Referees." *Time* (March 22, 1999): 91.

Beymer, Lawrence. *Meeting the Guidance and Counseling Needs of Boys.* Alexandria, VA: American Counseling Association, 1995.

Biddulph, Steve. *Raising Boys: Why Boys are Different & How to Help Them Become Happy and Well-Balanced Men.* Berkeley, CA: Celestial Arts, 1998.

Brooks, Robert, and Sam Goldstein. *Raising Resilient Children: Fostering Strength, Hope & Optimism in Your Children.* New York: McGraw-Hill, 2001.

Brusko, Marlene. *Living With Your Teenager.* New York: McGraw-Hill, 1986.

Coloroso, Barbara. *Kids Are Worth It: Giving Your Child the Gift of Inner Discipline.* New York: Avon Books, 1995.

Gardner, Howard. *Intelligence Reframed: Multiple Intelligences for the 21st Century.* Boulder, CO: Basic Books, 2000.

Ginott, Haim. *Teacher and Child.* New York: The Macmillan Company, 1972.

Grimes, Jeff, ed. *Psychological Approach to Problems of Children and Adolescents.* Des Moines: Iowa State Department of Public Instruction, 1982.

O'Brien, Lynn. *Learning Channel Preferred Checklist.* Potomac, MD: Specific Diagnostics, 1990.

Oster, Gerald D., and Sarah S. Montgomery. *Helping Your Depressed Teenager.* New York: John Wiley & Sons, 1994.

Parish, Thomas S., and Stanley E. Wigle. "A Longitudinal Study of the Impact of Parental Divorce on Adolescents' Evaluation of Self & Parents." *Adolescent* 20 (1985): 239–244.

Piaget, Jean, and Barbara Inhelder. *The Psychology of the Child.* Boulder, CO: Basic Books, 2000.

Ross, Dorothea M. *Childhood Bullying and Teasing.* Alexandria, VA: American Counseling Association, 1996.

Rubinstein, Carin. "The Children of Divorce as Adults." *Psychology Today* 13 (January, 1980): 74–75.

Ryckman, Richard M. *Theories of Personality*. Pacific Grove, CA: Brooks/Cole Publishing Co., 1993.

Silver, Larry. *Dr. Larry Silver's Advice to Parents on ADHD*. New York: Random House, Inc., 1999.

Sommers, Christina Hoff. *The War Against Boys*. New York: Simon & Schuster, 2000.

Taylor, John. *Helping Your Hyperactive/ADD Child*. Roseville, CA: Prima Publishing, 1997.

Walker, Doren J. *Pre-Adolescent Children's Reaction to Divorce*. Portales: Eastern New Mexico University, 1993.

Wallerstein, Judith S., and Joan B. Kelly, *California's Children of Divorce*. New York: *Psychology Today*, 1980.

Resources for Parents and Young Adolescents

ACHIEVEMENT

Heacox, Diane. *Up From Underachievement: How Teachers, Students and Parents Can Work Together to Promote Student Success*. Free Spirit Publishing, 2001.

Rosemond, John. *Ending the Homework Hassle: Understanding, Preventing and Solving School Performance Problems*. Andrews and McMeel, 1990.

Websites for Gifted Education

http://www.gtworld.org/.
http://www.hoagiesgifted.org/.

ANXIETY

Ross, Jerilyn. *Triumph Over Fear*. Bantam Books, 1995.

ATTENTION DEFICIT DISORDER (ADD)

Silver, Larry. *Dr. Larry Silver's Advice to Parents on ADHD*. Random House, Inc., 1999.

Taylor, John. *Helping Your Hyperactive/ADD Child*. Prima Publishing, 1997.

BOYS

Biddulph, Steve. *Raising Boys: Why Boys Are Different and How to Help Them Become Happy and Well-Adjusted Men*. Celestial Arts, 1998.

BULLYING

BBC Education: Bullying—A Survival Guide. http://www.bbc.co.uk/education/archive/bully/fact.html.

Bullying: What is It? http://www.successunlimited.co.uk/bully/bully.htm.

How to Help Your Child Avoid Violent Conflicts. http://www.uncg.edu/edu/ericcass/conflict/docs/ed387456.htm.

Langelan, M.J. *Back Off!: How to Confront and Stop Sexual Harassment and Harassers*. Simon & Schuster, 1995.

Ross, Dorothea M. *Childhood Bullying and Teasing*. American Counseling Association, 1996.

CAREERS

USA Today Education Site. http://www.education.usatoday.com.

COLLEGE

College Board. http://www.collegeboard.com.

O'Brien, Patrick. *Making College Count*. Graphic Management Corporation, 1996.

U.S. Department of Education's Project Cool. http://nces.ed.gov.

CONDUCT DISORDER

The Center for Mental Health Services. http://www.mentalhealth.org/cmhs/.

DEPRESSION

Oster, Gerald, and Sarah Montgomery. *Helping Your Depressed Teenager*. John Wiley and Sons, Inc., 1994.

DIVORCE

Ackerman, Marc J. *Does Wednesday Mean Mom's House or Dad's?* John Wiley and Sons, Inc., 1996.

Krementz, Jill. *How It Feels When Parents Divorce*. Alfred A. Knopf, 1988.

EATING DISORDERS

American Anorexia-Bulimia Association. http://www.aabainc.org.

GIRLS

Eagle, C.J., and C. Colman. *All That She Can Be: Helping Your Daughter Maintain Her Self-Esteem*. Fireside, 1994.
Pipher, Mary. *Reviving Ophelia*. Ballantine Books, 1995.

MENTAL HEALTH

Adolescence Directory on Line. http://education.indiana.edu/cas/adol/adol.html. From the Center for Adolescent Studies, Indiana University. Mental health issues, general health issues, counselor resources.

Adolescent Health On-Line. http://www.ama-assn.org/adolhlth/. The AMA's site with information for health care professionals, adolescents and their families.

American Academy of Child and Adolescent Psychiatry. http://www.aacap.org/. Helps parents and families understand development, behavioral, and mental health disorders affecting children, including adolescents.

American Psychological Association. http://www.apa.org/. This national organization provides a variety of material on mental health for adults and children.

National Institute of Mental Health. http://www.nimh.nih.gov.

MIDDLE SCHOOL

Farrell, Juliana, and Beth Mayall. *Middle School: The Real Deal*. 17th Street Productions, 2001.

PARENTING

About Teens. http://www.parentingteens.about.com/. A variety of information about parenting and adolescents. The Career Quest section of the site can give young adolescents career information. Gives young adolescents a preview of PSAT and SAT exams. Provides data on over 10,000 post secondary institutions with information on federal student aid program. Provides easy-to-read information about a variety of eating disorders.

Archives of Pediatrics and Adolescent Medicine. http://www.archpedi. ama-assn.org/. Targeted to health professionals, but articles on children's issues are of interest to parents. Fact sheet on Conduct Disorder in Children and Adolescents.

Brooks, Robert, and Sam Goldstein. *Raising Resilient Children: Fostering Strength, Hope and Optimism in Your Child.* McGraw-Hill, 2001.

Brusko, Marlene. *Living With Your Teenager.* McGraw-Hill, 1986.

Capuzzi, Dave, and Douglas R. Gross. *Youth At Risk.* American Association for Counseling and Development, 1999.

Cline, Foster, and Jim Fay. *Parenting Teens with Love and Logic.* Pinon, 1992.

Coloroso, Barbara. *Kids Are Worth It: Giving Your Child the Gift of Inner Discipline.* Avon Books, 1995.

Dinkmeyer, Don, and Gary McKay. *Parenting Teenagers.* American Guidance Service, 1998.

Fontenelle, Don H. *Keys to Parenting Your Teenager.* Barron's Educational Series, Inc., 1992.

Giannetti, Charlene C., and Margaret Sagarese. *Parenting 911.* Broadway Books, 1999.

Ginott, Haim G. *Between Parent and Child.* The Macmillan Company, 1965.

Kolodny, Dr. Robert C., Nancy J. Kolodny, Dr. Thomas Bratter, and Cheryl Deep. *How to Survive Your Adolescent's Adolescence.* Little, Brown and Company, 1984.

Parenting   Adolescents.   http://www.parentingadolescents.com/. Where parents can get free, extended, expert advice on parenting teens and preteens.

Renshaw Joslin, Karen. *Positive Parenting From A to Z.* Fawcett Colombine, 1994.

Schlessinger, Laura E. *Stupid Things Parents Do to Mess Up Their Kids: Don't Have Them if You Won't Raise Them.* Cliff Street Books, 2001.

Shalov, Jeanette, Irwin Spllonger, Jules Spotts, Phyllis Steinbrecher, and Douglas Thorpe. *You Can Say No to Your Teenager.* Addison-Wesley Publishing Company, Inc., 1998.

PEER RELATIONSHIPS

Schaeffer, Dick. *Choices and Consequences: What to Do When a Teenager Uses Alcohol/Drugs.* Johnson Institute Books, 1996.

Scott, Sharon. *How to Say No and Keep Your Friends.* Human Resource Development Press, Inc., 1997.

SELF-ESTEEM

Giannetti, Charles C., and Margaret Cliques Sagarese. *Eight Steps to Help Your Child Survive the Social Jungle.* Broadway Books, 2001.
Paulus, Trina. *Hope for the Flowers.* Paulist Press, 1997.
Silverstein, Shel. *The Missing Piece.* Harper Collins, 1987.

STRESS

Hipp, Earl, and Michael Fleishman (illustrator). *Fighting Invisible Tigers: A Stress Management Guide for Teens.* Free Spirit Publishing, 1995.
Robinson, Edward H., Mary Ann Fey, Joseph C. Rotter, and Kenneth R. Vogel. *Helping Children Cope with Fears and Stress.* Eric and Student Services Clearinghouse, 1991.

TEENS AND PARENTS

Family Haven. http://www.familyhaven.com. This site contains information on nutrition and adolescents and other educational material concerning the family and children in general.
Teenwire. http://www.teenwire.com. Run by Planned Parenthood, this resource for teenagers answers questions about sex, dating, and love.

Index

About the Author

EILEEN BERNSTEIN is Guidance Counselor at Gaithersburg High School, Maryland.